启 德 英 语 学 习 丛 书

轻松备战
雅思口语

曾健 编著

SPEAKING

中国水利水电出版社
www.waterpub.com.cn

内 容 提 要

本书系启德学府金牌口语教师力作，旨在帮助考生全方位备战雅思口语。

本书按照雅思口语考试过程划分，对三部分不同的题型、不同的题材，分门别类进行讲解。讲解得生动、全面，不仅点明了回答要点，而且补充了大量的词汇、句型和文化常识。为了丰富考生的思路，书中特别提供了阅读材料，有助于考生将问题回答得更精彩。

本书图文并茂、生动有趣、百读不厌，既是最佳雅思口语教材，也是优秀的自学手册。

本书适用于参加雅思口语考试的广大读者。

图书在版编目（ＣＩＰ）数据

轻松备战雅思口语 / 曾健编著. -- 北京 ：中国水
利水电出版社，2010.8（2014.4重印）
　　（启德英语学习丛书）
　　ISBN 978-7-5084-7758-9

　　Ⅰ．①轻… Ⅱ．①曾… Ⅲ．①英语－口语－高等教育
－自学参考资料 Ⅳ．①H319.9

中国版本图书馆CIP数据核字(2010)第149902号

书　　名	启德英语学习丛书 **轻松备战雅思口语**	
作　　者	曾健　编著	
出版发行	中国水利水电出版社 （北京市海淀区玉渊潭南路1号D座　　100038） 网址：www.waterpub.com.cn E-mail：sales@waterpub.com.cn 电话：（010）68367658（发行部）	
经　　售	北京科水图书销售中心（零售） 电话：（010）88383994、63202643、68545874 全国各地新华书店和相关出版物销售网点	
排　　版	美文苑文化发展有限公司	
印　　刷	北京嘉恒彩色印刷有限责任公司	
规　　格	184mm×245mm　16开本　12.5印张　297千字	
版　　次	2010年8月第1版　2014年4月第5次印刷	
印　　数	14001—17000册	
定　　价	38.00元（附光盘1张）	

凡购买我社图书，如有缺页、倒页、脱页的，本社发行部负责调换

版权所有·侵权必究

启德学府海外考试图书编委会核心小组

编委会主任：李　朱　　　　李碧燕　　　　管永川

特约策划人：吕　蕾

执 行 策 划：李碧燕

编　　　　委：启德学府海外考试研究中心

李碧燕　　　　余灼雅　　　　沈　栋　　　　莫　山

陈建仁　　　　冯结玲　　　　冯碧云　　　　杨宇霆

李　精　　　　陈文清　　　　邱蒲潇　　　　徐稳根

李　智　　　　罗秋萍　　　　文　静　　　　温文瑶

潘　夏　　　　杨曙光　　　　曾　健　　　　邓敏贤

陈松菁

致"烤鸭"语

本书的由来

作为曾经的"烤鸭"以及现任的雅思口语老师，笔者这几年陪伴着自己的学生经历了跌倒时的伤痛，也分享了无数学生成功时的喜悦。忙碌过后，安静下来的时候，总想把这一切点点滴滴都记录下来："烤鸭"们复习过程中的迷茫与无助，考试临近时的慌乱与担忧，等待成绩时的忐忑与不安……

经常有很多学生抱着沉甸甸厚如砖的雅思口语参考书来问笔者："Joedy啊，这本书好不好？怎么看？我背了答案怎么还是考得那么差？"

翻一翻这一堆的雅思参考书，大多数都是高高在上的权威说教式的辅导，学生在学习过程中被动地接受权威们写出来的答案，对于一些完美到不行的答案奉若神明，结果雅思考试成绩却未如预期理想。

看着学生迷茫与挫败的眼神，一个想法在笔者脑海中形成了：何不抛开一切的说教，以"烤鸭"的角度去记录一段真正属于我们自己的备考旅程呢？以"烤鸭"的口吻去总结我们的经验与教训，以"烤鸭"的笔触来记载我们的成长与收获，这样的书，应该更能切实帮助到学生放下所有包袱快乐备考吧？

这就是本书《轻松备战雅思口语》的由来。

本书的特点

书本里所有的题目来源于近一年的全真考题，保证了其真实性；所有问题的参考答案全部由我们的"烤鸭"提供，尽管不一定是完美的，但是极便于大家参考与模仿。

平时也欢迎大家登陆Joedy的雅思博客http://Joedy7.blog.163.com（早DD的小鸭天地），Joedy会就雅思口语的最新动态和"烤鸭"们进行交流。

学习应该是一个快乐的过程！来，现在就让Joedy陪伴你一起出发，踏上备考雅思的奇妙旅程，感受旅途中的所有惊喜和快乐吧！

我要感谢的人

另外，这本书最终得以出版，有太多感激的话要说：

感谢EIC，给我提供了一个广阔的平台，让我能够舒展拳脚；

感谢Simon，把我带进雅思教学这一充满惊喜的领域，不断督促我成长；

感谢Jennifer，给我树立了好榜样，总是为迷茫的我指明方向；

感谢花花，你适时的提点与支持，让我能够快速地进步；

感谢快D，总是在我快要放弃的时候，不断地鼓励与打气，让我有坚持的动力；

感谢Laura Feng（冯结玲）、Pat Feng（冯碧云）、Sandra Deng（邓敏贤）、Kathy Chen（陈猛）、Ellie、玲玲、辉仔，有了你们的支持和帮助，才有了这本书的最终出版。

Joedy

2010年7月于广州

目　录

第 1 章

认识

雅思口语考试

IELTS

第 *1* 节　雅思口语考试的形式与流程

雅思考试四部分当中，口语考试通常被很多"烤鸭"认为是最令人头痛和恐惧的一部分。下面是部分2008年全球雅思考生口语成绩统计表：

Mean band score by most frequent countries or regions of origin (Academic)

Source: www.ielts.org

Nationality	Speaking
Germany	7.24
Philippines	6.81
Russia	6.66
Malaysia	6.45
Italy	5.98
China's Hong Kong	5.93
Indonesia	5.86
Japan	5.80
Pakistan	5.79
India	5.77
Vietnam	5.72
Thailand	5.67
China's Taiwan	5.66
South Korea	5.60
China	5.25

要在雅思口语考试中取得理想成绩，有以下3个决定因素。

（1）"烤鸭"对于雅思口语考试的认识深与浅。

（2）"烤鸭"本身的英语口语基础高与低。

（3）"烤鸭"考前的针对性练习多与少。

但是，"烤鸭"备考雅思口语往往会走上两个极端。

（1）太把雅思口语当一回事了。

（2）太不把雅思口语当一回事了。

第1类的"烤鸭"对于自己的英文基础毫无信心，极度紧张，备考时过分追求"标准答案"，对于所见所闻一些所谓"好答案"奉若神灵，结果考试时给考官严重的背答案嫌疑；

第2类的"烤鸭"恰恰相反，他们对于自己的英文功底特别是口语特别自信，认为口语无非就是随便"侃"，根本无需考前作任何准备，结果考试时回答过于随意，东拉西扯，想到什么说什么，毫无逻辑性可言。

要真正在雅思口语考试中取得理想的分数，必须做到知己知彼，正所谓不打无准备的仗！所以，下面先来总体了解一下雅思口语考试的形式与流程。

1. 考试形式

雅思口语考试是考生与考官直接一对一的面对面交流，主要考查考生运用英语交流沟通的能力。考试的时间大约为11～14分钟，考试全程会由考官用MP3录音笔录下用以考试结束后的复查以确保考试的客观性。

2. 考试流程

雅思口语考试分为3个部分。

★ Part 1：（4～5分钟）一般性的简单问答

在这一部分里，考官首先会询问考生姓名、检查身份证；接着开启录音装置，考官报出考试名称、时间、地点、本人姓名；然后考官会通过提问的方式了解考生个人方面的一些情况，这些问题主要涉及家庭背景、家乡、学习与工作、生活习惯、兴趣爱好以及其他一些考生相对熟悉的一般性话题。例如：

Interviewer: Do you like music?

Candidate: Sure I do. I listen to music whenever I can and I especially like some soothing music which can help me unwire after a whole day's hard work.

★ Part 2：（3～4分钟）话题口头表述

在这个部分，考官会给考生一张话题提示卡(cue card)，要求考生就某个话题展开独立表述。提示卡一般包括以下几部分内容：主题(topic)，细节(details)，解释(explanation)。

看看下面这张示范卡。

Describe a game or sport you enjoyed playing when you were a child.

You should say:

What it was.

When you started playing it.

How you played it.

With whom you often played it.

And explain the reason why you liked playing it.

拿到提示卡后，考官会给考生一分钟的准备时间，考生可以利用这1分钟的时间迅速选好主题然后在考官提供的草稿上列好提纲，像下面这样：

Hide-and-seek

8 years old

{
park

seeker—cover eyes, count, look for

hiders—find the perfect place
}

with friends

{
fun

exciting

company
}

列好提纲后考生就要开始进行1.5～2分钟的口头描述了。

等描述完毕，有些考官还会根据考生表述的内容，追加1～2个直接相关的follow-up questions，对于这些问题，考生不必长篇大论，紧扣考官的问题简单作答即可。当然也有一些考官会什么都不问直接进入Part 3了。

Part 3：（4～5分钟）社会问题深入探讨

在此阶段，考官会根据考生在Part 2表述的内容，与考生进一步深入探讨与之相关的一些社会性的话题。例如，就Describe your best friend这一张Cue card，考官会问到以下问题：

a. In what different way do men and women make friends now?

b. Can the employers make friends with the employees?

c. What qualities does one need to make friends easily?

d. What influence does modern technology have on people's friendship?

在这一部分的测试过程中，考官会有意识地增加问题的难度深度、拓宽问题的涉及面、提高问题的灵活度。当然，考官还会根据考生的理解力来组织问题的内容和调整问题的难易程度。

考生在这个阶段的回答应该像是向考官论证自己的观点一样，应该更加具体更加充实，不能再像Part 1那样给出过于简练的回答了。在后面讲解Part 3真题时会给大家具体讲解如何展开论述，让自己的论证更加充实。

3．考试过程中考官使用的语言

★ 检查身份阶段

Good morning. Come in and take a seat.

My name is… and we'll talk about 11-14 minutes.

Can you tell me your full name, please?

What shall I call you?

Can I see your identification, please?

★ 第一部分Part 1

Now in this first part, I'd like to ask you some questions about yourself.

Let's talk about…

I'd like to move on now to talk about…

Let's change the topic…

★ 第二部分Part 2

Now I am going to give you a topic, and I'd like you to talk about it for one to two minutes. Before you talk, you'll have one minute to think about what you're going to say. You can make some notes if you wish. Do you understand?

Here is some paper and a pencil for making notes and here's your topic.

All right? Remember you have one to two minutes for this, so don't worry if I stop you. I'll tell you when the time is up. Can you start speaking now, please?

★ 第三部分Part 3

We've been talking about...and I'd like to discuss one or two more general questions related to this.

第2节　雅思口语考试的评分标准

雅思口语考试评分等级从1分到9分分成九个等级，评分的因素包括：

- Fluency and coherence 流利程度和连贯性
- Lexical resources and ability to use vocabulary effectively 词汇应用能力
- Grammatical range and accuracy 语法多样性与准确性
- Pronunciation 语音

以前的口语单项只有5、6、7分这样的整分，而不像阅读和听力单项那样存在着5.5或者6.5这样的半分，从2007年7月1日之后，口语引入了半分制度。

总地来说，中国考生大多数取得的雅思口语分数都介于4～7分之间，所以现在就4～7分这几个档次的具体要求作出简单的说明。

得分	评价指标
4分	语言能力仅限于基本的内容特别是熟知的领域； 交流中常有明显的停顿，时常有重复或自我更正，语意常有不连贯之处； 词汇选择上时常犯错，理解和表述上有很大困难，无法使用复杂结构； 发音总体给听者带来严重理解困难
5分	对于自己熟悉的领域，交流起来基本上没有问题； 能流畅表达简单语言，有时过多使用某些连接词或者语言中的信号词； 能讨论熟悉或不熟悉的话题，但词汇使用缺乏灵活性； 总是费劲地搜寻大脑中的词汇，特别是进入Part 3不熟悉的话题时即感吃力，无法展开探讨话题，只能表达大意； 能使用基本的句子结构，且使用基本正确，复杂结构通常包含错误，有时导致交流障碍
6分	有充分交流的意识，一般能清晰有效地运用语言； 有足够的词汇充分回答三个阶段的话题，虽然有时出现表达不准确、不恰当，或者出现理解偏差的地方。大致能使用同一语言的其他表达方式； 能使用连接词或语言中的信号词，尽管有时不正确； 能够理解和运用较复杂的语言，尤其是自己熟悉的领域，但缺乏灵活性；有时发音错误会给听者带来一点费解
7分	能充分展开，且没有刻意思考的痕迹，没有语言上的不连贯，能够灵活使用连接词或语言中的信号词； 能灵活使用丰富的词汇讨论多种话题，能使用较不常见的单词和习语，对语体和搭配有所了解，能有效使用同一语言其他表达方式； 能较灵活运用复杂的语言就一个话题进行较深层次的讨论； 母语语音对英语的影响极小，能使用多种语音手段来有效达意

第 2 章

备战

雅思口语考试

IELTS

如第一章提到的，要在雅思口语考试中取得理想成绩，有3个决定因素。

(1) "烤鸭"对于雅思口语考试的认识深与浅。

(2) "烤鸭"本身的英语口语基础高与低。

(3) "烤鸭"考前的针对性练习多与少。

在第一章已经帮助大家总体揭开了口语考试的面纱，但这仅仅是第一步。要真正取得雅思口语考试的成功，大家还要根据自身的口语基础以及能用于准备雅思口语考试的时间来定制属于自己的备考计划！

所以，接下来就结合雅思口语考试的考核内容以及大家的具体情况作好详细的作战方案。

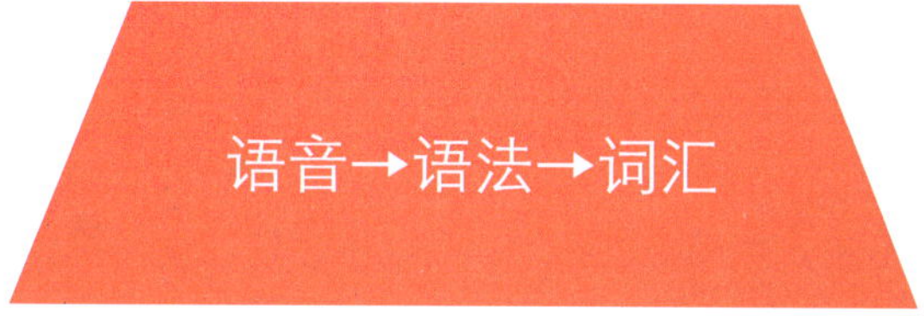

第1节　基础阶段

英语口语能力的根本提高不是一朝一夕就能够达到的。外语学习本来就是一个从量变到质变的漫长过程，所以本身底子比较弱的考生们，需先扎扎实实把基础打好。

那么基础从何打起呢？先补语法？还是先收集词汇？还是先补一下语音？先不要着急，让Joedy问大家一个很简单的问题：你自己在一开始跟某个人交流的时候，首先会注意到的是对方交流能力中的哪个方面呢？是这个人的词汇很丰富语法很厉害？或者是这个人的语音很漂亮交流很顺畅呢？

如果Joedy被问到这个问题，一定会不假思索地回答：当然是后者！

是的，如果要打个比方，语音就像是一个人的外表，语法和词汇就可以比作一个人的内涵。外表美会让自己更加自信，才能够吸引别人进一步了解自己的内涵。所以，大家现在先来好好打扮一下，穿上一件漂亮的语音外衣吧！

1. 语音：模仿是关键

雅思口语考试在2008年8月采用了新的口试发音评估量表，将从原来只有2，4，6，8分的4种分值的评分标准细化到9种。这样的口试发音评估会更精确地反映考生发音水平，更符合考生到了英语国家对发音和听力的要求，也更加实用化了，但也对考生提出了更高、更细的要求。

有的考生在备考过程中很担心，问道："我这种口音，考官会不会不喜欢？"其实，IELTS是international test system，根本没有所谓的"标准口音"。考官允许考生有口音，只要口音不影响到与考官的沟通，什么口音都OK。

那么，哪些发音方式会影响到与考官的沟通呢？以下从"音（Sound）、腔（Rhythm）、调（Intonation）"三大方面给大家列出考生普遍存在的问题。

（1）元音发音不到位。

（2）轻重音不分。

（3）结尾辅音吞音或者加音。

（4）不懂连读。

（5）句子停顿不当。

（6）语调过于平缓。

★ 跟读模仿

要想使自己的语音得到根本的改善，建议大家抛开一切的理论，每天抽出10～15分钟的时间，找一个安静的地方，开声跟读模仿《新概念英语2》里的任意一篇小文章。《新概念英语2》的故事篇幅不长，生词量也不大，很易于模仿。这种模仿不是随随便便地模仿，要务求直到自己发出来的音和原文录音一模一样为止才罢休，特别是刚刚提到的最容易出现问题的6个方面。如果现在的你对于自己的发音还是没有自信而导致不敢开声大胆表达自己，那就一定不能偷懒了，按照以下的步骤练习。

（1）先看一遍整个故事，理解整个故事情节，尝试自己先开声读一遍。

（2）放录音。听一句，暂停，然后学录音读一句，尽力模仿语音和语调。

（3）放下一句，暂停，再学一句，一直到最后。

（4）与录音同步朗读，跟上录音的速度和语调。

（5）关掉录音，朗读课文到极度熟练为止。

★ 开声朗读

就算你对自己目前的发音已经有足够的信心了，还是不能松懈。每天约10分钟的时间磨一下自己的嘴巴和舌头是很有必要的。大家可以选择一些简单的、易上口的文章，张开嘴巴开声把它美美地读出来，这是为了练习大家的舌头和口腔肌肉的灵活度，避免到时候明明准备得挺好的，开声才发现舌头不听话。我平时就特别喜欢拿起《21st century》对着镜子模仿新闻播音员的腔调读新闻，或者选择一篇《心灵鸡汤》里的动人故事尝试很有感情地对着镜子说出来。这方法虽然挺臭美的，但是过程中却是充满欣喜的。学习语言的最高境界不就是享受吗？试试吧。

2. 语法：光懂得语法知识是没有用的

雅思口语考试对于语法考查两个方面：语法知识面和语法准确性。语法知识面考查我们是否具备能够运用多种时态和多种语法结构进行表达的能力。语法准确性是看我们对动词时态、名词单复数、主谓一致等语法运用的准确性。

语法是被中国考生"妖魔化"了的一个语言考查点，除了对自己发音不自信，很多同学都因为害怕语法出错而不敢大胆地开口说英语。其实，就算对于一个母语为英语的人，日常交流中也会出现一些小错误，考官深明这个道理，所以对于考生的语法正确率不会太苛求。考官所关心的是语法错误对理解与交流所产生的影响，如果你的语法错误不足以影响交流的顺畅进行，那就大胆说吧！

★ 常见小错

平时大家应注意在交流中避免以下的低级小错误，这些小错误会干扰你和考官之间的交流。

错误1：	人称出错	例如"she"说成"he"，"he"说成"it"
错误2：	主谓单复数出错	例如"He doesn't"说成 "He don't"，"I am"说成"I is"
错误3：	时态出错	例如"I went to school."说成"I go to school."

★ 常用关联词

有些考生提出："我在交流中使用一些复杂结构，应该会让考官眼前一亮吧？会增加分数吗？"是的。交流中适当地混合使用简单句型和复杂句型，的确是让自己的表达显得灵活一些。问题是，很多考生都把复杂句等同于从句了。其实，复杂结构不一定就是从句结构，如果考生能在交流中灵活使用一些关联词，也会让自己的语法结构显得复杂。一些常用的关联词包括：

（1）表递进：and, then, also, besides, plus

（2）表转折：but, though, yet, still

（3）表因果：so, because, since, as

（4）表条件：if, whether, unless, as long as

（5）表举例：such as, for example, like

★ 给自己犯错的机会

要克服语法大关，我们不需要去刻意学习系统的语法知识，其实光知道正确的语法知识是没有用的，最重要的是我们如何把语法知识用到真正的交流中来。不要因为害怕犯错而杜绝开口，恰恰相反，我们应该多创造机会听到自己的错误。只有这样，我们才能意识到自己最常犯的错误有哪些。同学们平时可以多尝试用MP3录下自己讲出来的话，例如，用两分钟的时间描述一个自己的好朋友。回头听听自己的录音，检查一下有没有把"she"说成"he"啦？有没有弄错了单复数呢？有没有混乱了时态？经过不断地犯错不断地自我检查，我相信，大家的错误会越来越少。记住，最重要的是给自己机会去犯错！

3. 词汇：需要什么词就收集什么词

雅思口语考试到底需要掌握多少单词？相信很多考生心中都有这样的疑问。其实，在口试中，考官根本无法确切了解考生的词汇量究竟有多大，事实上也没有这个必要，考官重点要考查的是考生是否能准确而恰当地运用词汇清晰达意。具体考查点有以下四点。

★ 用词是否准确

常见的错误是按照中文的习惯硬译英文，例如"turn on TV"说成"open TV"；"read the newspaper"说成"see the newspaper"。

★ 用词是否自然恰当

常见的问题是套用大量的正式书面用语以及深奥的大词，例如"additionally" "consequently" "In conclusion"。

★ 用词是否丰富多变

考生经常会滥用一些词汇，例如"beautiful" "friendly" "like" "good"等，导致有考官发出感慨：It seems that all Chinese are friendly and all Chinese hometowns are beautiful.

★ 是否懂得避开词汇障碍

考生在考前不可能把所有需要的单词全部都收集完，由于词汇量有限，在考试时往往找不到合适的词语去表达自己想表达的意思。就算收集了所有需要的词汇，考试时因为紧张，也会出现突然脑子空白什么都想不起来的情况。这个时候该怎么办呢？考生大可不必那么快就轻言放弃或者回避问题，可以采取积极的交流策略，避难就易：

☆ 换简单表达或者同义词

例如"Hong Kong is the world famous shopping paradise."如果实在想不起来paradise怎么说，有没有更简单一点的方法可以替代这个词呢？这个时候，考生大可以用place 或者centre去迅速填补这个空白，千万不要为了这么一个词而停在那里什么都不说。记得一个考官说过的：Don't say what you want to say. Say what you can say.

☆ 适当使用母语

有些表达根本不需要太执著去寻找他们相应的英文表达，保留一点他们原来的味道有时也是个不错的方法。例如广州著名的珠江（Pearl River），如果记不住Pearl River，大可说"The famous river in Guangzhou, Zhujiang."，考官知道考生讲的Zhujiang就是一条河，那么，沟通目的已经达到了。

☆ 列出具体的例子

例如，当考生想说"我最喜爱的食物就是水果"的时候，偏偏就记不起来"水果(fruit)"怎么说了，这个时候可以这么说：My favorite kind of food is things like apples and bananas.

所以啊，遇到不懂的单词并不可怕，可怕的是大家不会去变通。考生只需收集一些基本的必须的单词和表达，够用就好！那么怎么样去收集一些基本的必须的单词和表达呢？

雅思口语考试的内容都是紧紧围绕着社会民生最新最热门的话题，所以考生平时要多关注社会性的一些话题。大家平时可以多上Joedy的雅思博客http://Joedy7.blog.163.com，Joedy会定期更新最新的雅思口语热门话题，大家可以根据Joedy提供的热门话题，针对性地去收集自己需要的一些单词。例如，当考生需要回答一个这样的题目：What kind of music do you like? 需要用到的单词和表达可能有classical music, jazz, R&B等，不需要全部都收集，只需收集自己所需要的那个表达就可以了！

第2节　培训阶段

打好了基础后，同学们可以考虑在考前2～3个月参加一个好的雅思培训班，这些课程一般安排得比较紧凑，在这种浓厚的学习氛围下，能让考生在较短的时间内迅速熟悉雅思考试模式并找到志同道合的学习伙伴。最重要的是，培训班的老师大多对考试最新动态非常熟悉，可以给我们提出针对性的建议。接下来先来熟悉一下雅思口语考试的常用技巧吧！

1. Part 1（4～5分钟）一般性的简单问答

在这一部分里，考官会通过一些简单的问答让考生热身并且迅速进入状态，考官问的问题都是一些考生相对熟悉的一般性话题。现在选取一段口语考试的真实过程来给大家作点评分析，让大家了解一下Part 1到底具体是怎样考的。

C = Candidate　　　I = Interviewer

人物	问答	评论
I	Good morning! Come in and take a seat. My name is Susan. Could you tell me your full name, please?	考官与考生打招呼并介绍自己名字，然后询问考生名字，帮助考生轻松进入交流状态
C	My name is Li Hong, and you can call me by my English name Laura.	简单明了介绍自己的全名和英文名
I	May I see your identification, please?	检查考生身份

（续表）

人物	问答	评论
C	Ok, here you go.	简单作答即可
I	Now in this first part, I'd like to ask you some questions about yourself. Let's talk about your hometown. What kind of place is it?	hometown是一个很常见的话题，几乎每个考生都会遇到
C	OK, I was born and raised in Dalian. It is a beautiful city all year round and it enjoys fine weather.	直接作答，作适当的扩展
I	What is the most interesting part in Dalian?	考官进一步提问了解情况
C	Its beaches. They are famous in China because they are quite clean. They attract many visitors every year.	一点扩展到底，对beaches的特点深入描述
I	Now let's move on to talk about what you like doing in your spare time. Do you have any hobbies or interest?	hobbies也是很常见的话题，能帮助对方很好地了解考生
C	Yes, I enjoy going shopping a lot. It is really fun. But it's just window shopping for me most of the time, because you know… er… shopping is expensive. I cannot afford that all the time.	具体表达自己的喜好，对自己的喜好作出一定的解释说明

*J*oedy 提醒：

Part 1涉及的问题一般都比较简单，而且这一阶段是第一印象形成的绝佳时期，大家要记得要尽快进入状态，从容作答。

※态度积极

充分积极回应考官问题，绝对不要问一句答一个词而已或者对考官选定的话题避而不答。要尽量提供具体与有效的信息 (to be specific and informative)。

※回答自然

不要长篇大论，自然作答就好。其实这一阶段主要是为了热身与放松，让考生初步展示基本的英文口头表达能力，所以大家记得千万不要给考官留下背答案的嫌疑。

*P*art 1 小策略：

问题1：听不清问题怎么办？

假如听不清楚或者听不懂考官的问题，不要回避，要尽量积极主动地回应考官。我们可以礼貌地向考官提出请求，例如：

Sorry, I didn't quite follow you. Can you repeat the question?

Sorry, I missed the word after "the". Can you say that again?

Sorry, I am not sure the meaning of the word.

Would you mind putting it in another way?

Sorry, I don't quite understand the word… Can you rephrase it?

So you are saying that…

Do you mean that…?

问题2：不懂扩展答案怎么办？

按照考生平时交流中最喜欢追问的两类问题，当不懂得如何扩展时，都可以尝试用总分总的回答方式，也就是：

总体作答→扩展（原因/具体信息/举例）→圆场（重申观点/表达感受）

※客观类信息题 (e.g. Where do you come from?)

这类题目考官要求考生向考官提供客观的信息，考生应该提供足够的信息，才不至于让考官不断追问，考生的回答模式可以是：General information + detailed information

所以可以这样答：

I am from Maoming, a medium-sized city in the eastern part of Guangdong. It is a coastal city and the beaches there are really fabulous.

通过扩展自己的答案，考官对于考生的家乡有个初步的了解了，这个简单的交流就成功了。记住，绝对不要问一句答一句。

※主观类意见题 (e.g. Do you like music?)

这类题目考生需要就某个问题向考官表达自己的态度，并且对于自己的观点适当地加以解释，要把自己的观点解释清楚，考官才不至于产生疑问。这类问题的回答模式可以是：Opinion + Reason + (Example)

所以对于Do you like music?这个问题，可以这样答：

Yes, I love it especially some soothing music, because it can always help me to get some inner peace. Sometimes when I feel totally wiped out after a whole day's hard work, music can let me calm down at once.

问题3：突然停顿了怎么办？

有时考官问的问题一下子把考生难倒了，不知道该如何是好，或者有时因为紧张，突然脑子一片空白。这个时候怎么办呢？总不能就这样两个人停在那里啊！考生要学会用一些话语去填补那个尴尬的空白，让交流显得还是顺畅的，常见的填补空白的话语有：

Well, actually…

Wow, that's difficult.

Let me see.

As a matter of fact,

How shall I put it?

I mean…

总之，就是把当时心里所有在思考的过程用语言表达出来就好啦。这样，才不至于让考官以为考生突然脑子短路了。

问题4：不会回答怎么办？

有时考官问到的一些问题刚好是考生平时不多关注的或者根本就不感兴趣的方面。这个时候不要那么快就灰心丧气，有个考官说过："I don't care about how you answer the question. All I want to know is how you respond to my question. It's not what you say. It is how you say it." 也就是说，答案不是考官追求的，考官只想通过考生回答问题来展示自己的语言能力。所以，就算不知道所谓正确答案也不要紧，只要给出适当的反应，展示了语言能力，一样能取得胜利。例如：

Interviewer: Is riding bicycle popular in your hometown?

Candidate: Sorry, I don't know for sure, because it's been 10 years since I moved to Guangzhou. But I guess it might be popular in my hometown because I once saw a picture of my hometown in which many people were riding bicycles.

在以上回答中，考生首先承认自己对这个问题不是太清楚，接着给出了一个合理的理由解释自己为什么不清楚。最妙的是在最后，考生还积极地根据自己的经验作出猜测，尽管这个猜测不一定是真实的。这种积极回应考官问题的态度会受到考官的认可的，大家大胆尝试吧！没有任何题目可以难倒大家！

2. Part 2（3-4分钟）话题口头表述

结束了Part 1对话之后，通常考官会说Well, I guess it's time to move to the next stage. 直接把考生带进Part 2去。在这一阶段，考官会给考生一张Cue card（话题提示卡）、一支笔和一本草稿本，以及用以打草稿的一分钟准备时间。很多同学都觉得，那一分钟的时间太短了，而要讲两分钟的时间又太漫长了。要怎么样去好好利用那一分钟，然后让自己的2分钟变得精彩呢？接下来用一张最近考得很热门的Cue card和大家分享一下。

Describe an interesting speech/lecture you attended.

You should say:

What it is about

Where you attended it

Who gave the speech/lecture

And explain why you think it is interesting.

Part 2 小策略：

> 问题1：一分钟时间怎么利用？

首先，花5秒钟的时间找出卡片上的关键词。

哪些才是关键词呢？关键词应该是能帮助考生确定主题以及主旋律的词，如果关键词看错了，很容易就会走题或者偏题了。所以，建议大家一定要找好以下两种关键词：

※第一行的中心名词 (i.e. speech/lecture)

※中心名词前后的修饰语 (i.e. interesting)

原来，这一次考生要讲的是一个speech，而且要突出这个speech里interesting的一面。看，找好了关键词，主题以及中心就定下来了。

接着，花25秒钟选好主题搭好框架。

确定了主题后，考生要开始选好自己要讲的内容以及迅速搭好框架。考生可以在草稿本上写下简单的草稿，如：

how to keep healthy

at school

famous doctor

interesting

最后，花30秒钟扩充组织自己的语言。

光光是写了上面那么一丁点草稿，很多同学几句话就讲完了，根本不可能扩展成2分钟。所以，最后30秒考生一定要思考如何扩展语言。

※找好扩充点，加上详细描述或者具体实例

扩充点可以因人而异，每个考生所选择的角度都可以不一样。像这张卡片，最容易也最应该扩展的地方当然就是interesting了，所以可以在interesting那个点上加上具体的细节描述，加以扩展。

※必要时还可以把key words排一下顺序

有些时候如果考生觉得按照原来卡片给出的顺序太过死板的话，可以在草稿原文上加上标志加以排序。但是这个步骤不是必须的。

- how to keep healthy

- at school

- famous doctor

- interesting { lots of pictures / interesting story / activity }

在接下来的2分钟时间里面，考生要怎样才能打动考官呢? 建议大家要注意以下几点：

※流畅性

Part 2的陈述就像是一个口头命题作文一样，行云流水般的描述，才会让听者感到愉悦。考生要保证自己在Part 2不要结结巴巴断断续续，平时就要多点保持语感锻炼，多点尝试限制自己2分钟之内描述眼前所见的一切，包括一个电视节目啊，一瓶饮料啊，一件衣服啊，一本杂志啊，一个广告啊，一栋楼啊……慢慢养成随口描述事物的习惯。

※准确性

在2分钟的时间里，考官是一个听众，全程在听着考生论述，考生就像是在向一个听众作演讲一样。如果我们在讲话过程中频繁让听众听到一些低级幼稚的错误，那实在是大煞风景呢! 所以在陈述过程中要尽量减少低级的小错误，例如人称要搞清楚啦，不要把father说成是she啦，把girlfriend说成he啦。平时可以多点用MP3录下自己的2分钟描述，回头去听听自己有没有因为紧张而出现一些原则性的错误，例如人称、单复数和时态，假如发现在某一方面频繁出错，就要多加注意修正，保证下次不再犯同样的错误了。

※生动性

说到生动性，想要谈到以下两点：

生动性1：联系个人经历，讲述个人的真实情感

考官一天要测试好多考生，如果每个人走进考场都给考官几乎一致的答案，考官会感觉了无生趣。那是不是说一定要给出标新立异的答案呢? 不是的，考生要做的是：联系自己的个人经历，讲述自己的真实情感，用自己的真实感受去打动考官。

考生平时要养成"讲故事"的习惯，故事是最容易拉近与考官之间的距离的。试问谁不喜欢听故事呢? 就算是考官都不例外。

例如，当考生要描述a sports event you saw or attended的时候，根本不需要去挑选"奥运会"或者"世界杯"这些离自己很遥远的sports event来描述，考生可以选择自己学校班级之间的一场篮球比赛啊，然后具体描述这场篮球比赛中同学们的真实感受。比起用很虚幻的语言去介绍奥运会的来历和常识，这样的平淡而真实的描述，更能打动考官。

生动性2：非语言因素要到位

当然啦，要打动听众，单纯用语言是不够的。就像是一份一模一样的演讲稿，两个不同的演讲者演讲，会得出截然不同的效果。因为两者给自己的陈述辅以了不同的非语言因素。所谓的非语言因素包括了眼神交流、表情和肢体语言。

很多考生在陈述过程中过多注意自己的用词是否精确，语法是否正确，时间是否足够……结果导致目光呆滞、表情木讷、肢体僵硬，考官这时很有可能会怀疑考生在背原来已经准备好的答案。这样就算考生的答案非常完美，也是大打折扣了的。

所以平时练习时要多注意自己的非语言因素。考生可以在练习讲故事时多对着镜子，看看自己的表情和动作是否得体，看看自己是否能够给予自然的眼神接触。这会给考生的论述锦上添花，试试吧！

※逻辑性

我们判断一个人语言表达好与坏，不单单是看他是否能很流利地说话，还要看这个人的逻辑性。所谓逻辑性，体现在以下几个方面：

逻辑性1：前后衔接是否自然

很多考生在Part 2不习惯打草稿，这个习惯一定要改正。打草稿能够帮助考生快速地梳理陈述的条理，避免到时候东拉西扯不知所云。考生不需要写很详细的草稿，简单的自己能看得懂的就OK啦。例如，对于以下这张卡片，试着写个简单的草稿，并且按照自己的逻辑顺序编排草稿的顺序。

> Describe a person you enjoy spending most time with.
>
> You should say:
>
> > Who this person is.
> >
> > How you met this person.
> >
> > What kind of person he/she is.
> >
> > What you usually do together.
>
> And explain the reason why you like spending time with him/her.

①Chloe

②university

③kind

⑥Considerate ｛ last year

I broke up with my bf, heartbroken, lost confidence

④Shopping

comfort, accompany, help get through the hard time

⑤sharing

真正在考试的时候，考生的草稿不需要那么详细那么具体，尽量精简一点清晰一点就可以了。只要有纲可循就可以啦！

逻辑性2：重点是否突出

除了前后衔接条理要清晰之外，还要让自己的陈述显得重点突出。就像写作文的时候，一定要有高潮才能吸引读者。

考生在陈述时不需要每一个要点都扩展，只需找一个侧重点重点扩展就可以，就像上面的示范介绍好朋友Chloe一样，只需重点去扩展Chloe的considerate的一面就好啦，其他的方面就迅速带过去就可以了。只有这样，考官才会觉得我们说话是有重点(point)的。

很多同学都担心："我在考试的时候如果遇到一张从来都没有准备过的卡片，一时无语，怎么办啊?"像2008年5月新出了一张卡片要求考生讲a good law in your country，大家又不是法律专业的，事实上考生在考前无论多努力准备，都有可能会遇到新卡。在考前准备完所有的卡片是很不实际的，只需具体准备几张最具代表性的卡片，就足够应付所有的卡片了。例如，我有个学生考前就准备了一张卡片impressive journey，具体内容是这样的：

Now I would like to share with you an impressive journey I took three years ago to a remote village called Ningfeng near Beijing city. I went there with two close friends and we stayed there for about half a month. In Ningfeng, we enjoyed the most peaceful life that we had never had in our life back in the city. What makes the trip so unforgettable is that we met a teacher in the village, Mr. Shi. He is the only college student in Ningfeng and after graduation, he returned to his hometown and began teaching in the primary school of the village. Families in this poor village cannot afford school and parents were reluctant to send their children to school thinking that it was a waste of money and time. Many children had to quit school early and helped their parents with the farm work. Mr. Shi tried all he could to keep the school running and helped children to continue with their studies while he himself was leading a hard life and suffering from bad stomachache. We were greatly touched by what Mr. Shi had been doing and talking to him was really inspiring. I had never thought that one could actually sacrifice so much to help others. I realized how lucky I was and how self-centered I had been. I do hope that I can also do something to help. After we left and came back to our city, I decided to donate some money every year and support one child to go back to school. So, that's the most impressive journey I would like to share with you.

好了，有了这张经典卡，大家可以开始来变身了。

假如考生看到一张卡片describe a person who is good at his/her job，就可以讲Mr. Shi了；见到the place you most want to go in the world的话，那就是Ningfeng了，可以说现在想去看看这几年的变化；如果是an important letter you received的话，可以说是收到的Mr. Shi寄过来的一封感谢信就好啦；就算是a good law in your country也没有问题啊，就说九年义务教育法，因为亲身在Ningfeng见到贫困山区的孩子过的艰苦日子，这个法律当然是很好了；如果要讲an important change in your life，也可以讲Ningfeng的经历啊，的确是让自己有所改变。

其实就算见到再多的新卡，大家只要稍微把经典卡改头换面，就几乎没有什么类型的卡片是没法转过去的，最重要的是要善于去发现卡与卡之间的微妙关联。我会在后面的真题点评章节里再具体跟大家讲解是如何让自己的经典卡千变万化的。

3. Part 3 （4～5分钟）社会问题深入探讨

Part 2结束后，考官接着会与考生就Part 2卡片的话题内容展开深层次的讨论，这个阶段的问题是由Part 2引申出来的一些社会性话题，要求考生能就某个特定话题表达自己的见解来论证自己的观点。Part 3是中国学生觉得最难的部分，在这一部分要和考官达到真正意义上的探讨，考生的思维模式要做到以下两点：

要点1: 观点鲜明，勿模棱两可

我们的教育一直都倡导想问题要全面，不能太片面，要用辩证的思维看世界。这令考生在回答口语问题时总是在酝酿最全面最完美的答案，很多同学无论被问到什么问题，都喜欢说：It depends. It is hard to say. Every coin has two sides. 其实，口语交流根本就不存在一个完美的标准答案，答案没有错误与正确之分。对于同一个问题，初中生有初中生的角度，专家有专家的角度，只要从考生自己的角度真诚地与考官交流，就足够了，不需要摇摆不定东拉西扯。

要点2: 论据充足，勿满口大道理

Part 3考官除了考查考生表达观点的能力，还要求考生有论辩、分析和归纳的能力。论证的方式有几种：讲道理（解释原因）、摆事实（举实例论证）、谈后果（举反例论证）。例如回答Is it necessary for us to spend more time with our family members?这个问题的时候，可以用三种方式来论证多和家人在一起的重要性。

> **讲道理**: Yes, it is necessary for us to spend time with our family because it gives us good opportunity to communicate with our family members and improve our relationship.
>
> **摆事实**: Yes, it is important for us. Take my family for example, we often try to find some time to get together. It really makes us closer. Like last weekend, we took a short trip to the suburbs, we did enjoy ourselves.
>
> **谈后果**: Yes, it is crucial for us to spend more time with our family, or we will feel more and more drifted apart. My father is busy with his work and he is not at home often. We don't have much time to be together and I feel it hard to communicate with him.

这里考生最大的问题是，长期以来大家都习惯于用"讲道理"的方法去论证，在论证过程中根本找不到可以支持自己论点的实际内容，结果只能啰啰嗦嗦翻来覆去讲述同一个大道理，无法做到真正意义上的论证观点。而西式的思维习惯中，往往注重事实论证，正所谓Facts speak louder than words.（事实胜于雄辩）。

现在就Part 3常见的几种问题类型和大家讲讲如何养成"摆事实"论证的习惯：

※ 描述类

描述类的问题要求考生对某个事物的客观现状进行描述。例如：

What is the impact of modern technology on people's life?

考生可以先对现代科技的影响作一个总体的描述，然后直接用具体事实去支撑观点就可以了，不需要解释原因，思路可以是：

General description + detailed description + Examples

所以，可以这样回答：I guess the impact is mainly positive.（总体描述）Modern technology has made our life more and more convenient.（进一步细化描述）I remember several years ago, if I wanted to contact my friends who lived in other cities, I needed to send letters. It usually took me a whole week to receive their reply. But things are much easier now. I can choose to send e-mails, which will take me about seconds, or phone our friends directly.（举具体事实证明）Modern technology is really bringing us a more comfortable life.（回应自己的观点）

※分析类

有时考官会让考生分析一些社会现存的问题，考官通常比较关心的社会问题有以下几类：

- 环保问题(environment)
- 交通问题(traffic)
- 老年人问题(the elderly)
- 儿童成长问题(children)
- 传统文化问题(traditional culture)
- 健康问题(health)
- 工作与就业问题(career and employment)
- 现代媒体的影响问题(modern media)

就以上那么多问题，只要大家平时多看、多观察、多积累各方面的社会话题以及从自己的角度多思考，就可以形成自己的观点了。可以用这种方式来回答：

Situation + details of the situation + (cause) + Examples

为什么在cause那里打了个括号呢？也就是说，原因分析不是必须的。虽然考官让考生分析问题，但考生毕竟不是专家，没有必要一定要分析社会问题的成因，如果实在不知道具体的原因，大可不必为难自己，直接用事实去告诉考官就可以了。例如这个问题：

How is the traffic situation in most big cities in your country?

考生可以这样回答：Well, I should say it is not so good.（直接道出现状）In most cities especially big cities such as Guangzhou and Shenzhen, traffic jams occur all the time. Sometimes we are stuck on the bus for about one hour and we can do nothing about it.（进一步具体描述现状）The other night when a heavy rain stroke Guangzhou, we were caught in the jam for two hours. That is really horrible.（举出一个实例论证）

※解决类

分析完问题后，考官一般都会关注考生如何解决这个社会问题。如果考官不问这个问题的成因，考生也不必去分析原因，直接给考官提供一个可行的解决方案就好。大致的回答思路可以是这样：

Solution + details of the solution + Examples

注意，往往一想到solution，就会想到government，经常听到同学们给出很敷衍的解决方案：I think the government should take some measures to solve this problem.这样的答案考官已经能背出来了，是完全没有意义的。希望大家要给出一个有诚意的解决方案，也就是要让考官看得到这个solution的可行性，越具体越好，不要空口说大话。

一般说来，无论责任是government的还是individuals的，谈到解决方案，大家都可以往两方面想一下：①物质；②精神。

例如这个问题：How can we solve the traffic problems in the cities?

考生可以从自己的角度这样答：Actually there are many ways of solving this problem and I guess the most effective way is to encourage people to use more public transport.（提出具体解决方案）Our government can make it cheaper and more comfortable for people to take the public transport.（进一步从物质上提出具体解决方案）For example, people can enjoy a discount if they take the bus regularly in a month.（举实例支撑自己的观点）

※态度类

考生经常需要在Part 3表达自己的观点表明自己的态度，这一类的问题回答思路比较简单：

Opinion + Reason + Examples

例如，当考官问考生：Do you believe the news reports on the media?

可以这样回答：No, not really.（直接表明态度）I don't think they are all telling the truth. Some journalists overstate what has happened in order to attract our attention.（陈述原因）Last week a news report on a magazine said that the famous HK star Andy Lau got married finally. Later I found out it wasn't the truth.（举实例）So I don't always believe what I read on the newspaper or the magazine.（重申观点）

※展望类

Part 3的探讨经常牵涉到回望过去与展望将来。我发现很多同学在展望将来的时候总是顾虑很多并且自我否定："我这么预测考官会不会觉得可笑啊？好像这样预测不大可能吧？"

其实同学们大可不必顾虑那么多，教大家一个小窍门，凡是要大家展望某事物将来的发展，大家就看看现在该事物的现状是什么，有什么缺陷，然后大胆去预测将来该事物的发展就好了。因为我们人类的生活都是在不断地克服现在的不足而向前发展的，所以大家就大胆预测吧！考生的思维方式可以这样：

Trend + Current situation + (cause) + Examples

例如，当考生被问到：How will the Internet develop in the future?

可以这样回答：Well, I guess the Internet in the future will be more and more multi-functional（预测将来发展方向）with the development of modern technology.（简单陈述原因）For example, when I am doing online shopping, I can not only see the products, but also touch and smell them.（举例子）

※对比类

对比两事物的区别是每次Part 3必考的问题类别，一般考官都会要求考生对比以下几组：

Males	East	Young	Now	Team	Family
Females	West	Old	Past	Individuals	Friends

在回答对比类问题的时候，很多同学容易头脑混乱。毕竟两个事物之间的差别可以体现在很多方面，例如当考官问道：What are the differences between newspapers and magazines?的时候，考生脑子里会涌进很多想法，例如：价钱有差别，出版周期有差别，目标读者群有差别，内容侧重点有差别……其实大家不必回答得那么全面，只需重点突出一点就OK了！可以用这种方式：

Standard + Differences + Examples

考生可以先告诉考官要侧重对比什么，然后重点去对比那一点就OK了！例如可以这样回答：Well, actually there are many differences between newspapers and magazines, and I guess the biggest difference lies in their content.（把所有的区别梳理成一点侧重提出）The information on the newspapers is very general while what the magazines contain is rather professional.（具体提到两者之间的区别）Take Guangzhou Daily and National Geographic for example. They are totally different. We can read almost all kinds of information on Guangzhou Daily whereas we can mainly get information about geography on National Geographic.（举实例）So I think the main difference is the content.（回应观点）

好了，讲到这里，大家对于"摆事实"论证的方式是不是有了一定的概念了呢？

其实，论据是需要积累的。就像一个能侃侃而谈的人，肯定是一个平时对周围的事情都能留心观察的人。论据是靠收集的，平时大家可以练习收集以下论据。

※媒体的报道以及调查的数据

数据和报道是说服力最强的论据，如果大家平时能收集到一些这些论据，那就最好。可以多看报纸，例如《21st Century》，里面有大量的报道和论据供大家收集，即使不是英文报纸，中文报纸里的头版或者社评版也是很好的论据来源。例如当考生被问到"Do Chinese people place much importance on getting together with family members？"时，可以用一个数据说明问题：

Yes, we surely do. According to a survey recently taken, around 95.7% Chinese go back home to spend the Chinese new year with the family no matter how busy they are. During the snow disaster last January, almost 600,000 train passengers who were eager to go home for the Spring Festival holiday were stranded.

看，数字的威力好大吧！极好地证明了中国人到底有多重视与家人团聚。

※自己的亲身经历

如果大家没办法收集到一些数据和报道，那么只能通过自己的亲身经历去向考官论证自己的观点了，这叫"以身说法"。尽管这样有一定的片面性，但是引用个人经历的论证也能很好地拉近考生和考官的距离。

例如，就刚才那个问题"Do Chinese people place much importance on getting together with family members？"考生可以引用自己的经历这样答：

Well, I don't know about others. But as far as I know, I think yes. Take my family for example, we will get together and have a big dinner every week no matter how busy we are. During some important festivals such as the Chinese New Year, we even gather with our relatives and have a big feast at the restaurant. It is so much fun and we feel warm.

※"捏造"事实

假如考官问的方面与考生的亲身经历没有任何交集，大家也不必慌张。可以运用自己的常识，编造一个无伤大雅的小谎言，让自己的论据显得更加充分。例如，考官问：Is swimming beneficial for children? 就算考生自己本身没有这方面的数据，而且自己也没有学习过游泳，考生还是能有自己的观点的，可以这么说：

Yes, swimming is absolutely important for children especially for their health. （总体观点）My little cousin was quite weak before and I often heard that he caught bad cold. Last year my uncle sent him to a swimming class and he began learning it. After a few months, I could see his changes. He becomes stronger and healthier. （捏造一个事实作为论据）So I think swimming really does a lot of good to children especially to their bodies. （回应观点）

第 3 节　冲刺篇

好了，基础打好了，技巧培训课也上完了，后面应该给自己预留约一个月的时间去充分巩固自己的基础和技巧！毕竟大家到时候是与考官一对一面对面地交流，与考官那么近距离地交流，很多同学都会怯场。考前所有要注意的要点一见到考官就全忘记了，极大地影响了自己的发挥，所以考前要进行大量的模拟练习以适应这种紧张的感觉。

1.　临考前模拟练习

方法1：与同学或者外国朋友练习

如果大家要找同学或者外国朋友练习，可不能随随便便找。这个朋友或同学必须要了解雅思的考试流程以及评分标准，而且大家要根据某个话题集中练习，这样才能够避免练习的盲目性，最大限度帮助自己往正确的方向改进。不然，很容易会导致交流的随意性过强，变成纯粹的free talk了。

方法2：找有经验的老师指导

大家可以到培训中心找懂雅思的外教来面对面模拟，如果没有外教，中教也可以。其实我的学生都普遍反映，中国老师的技巧性会比外教来得更强一些。

方法3：自练自说

如果找不到伙伴与自己练习，其实自己也可以进行模拟。大家只需准备三件工具：镜子、MP3、最新热门考题。可以每天花15分钟的时间，面对着镜子，练习最新的口语话题，练习全程用MP3录下自己的回答。

对着镜子的目的是让大家更好地练习自己的非语言因素包括肢体语言，面部表情之类的，而且还能让大家养成直面一个人的眼神迅速作答的习惯。而用MP3录音也能够促使大家快速作答而不至于拖拖拉拉，录完之后还可以回头听听自己的表达是否有一些不流畅或者低级小错误的出现。

所以就算是自己，也没有问题，最重要的是，不要给自己借口偷懒！

2.　考前一天

OK，经过了一段时间的打基础、学技巧以及临考模拟，大家终于要上战场了。到了考前的24小时，应该做些什么呢？这个时候不需要再去做过多的练习了。只会越复习越心慌越发现有好多都没有准备呢！大家跟着我走好以下几步吧！

练习1：活动口腔，保持语感

临考前一天特别是考前那几小时，大家要多活动活动嘴巴开开声说英语。毕竟雅思口语考试只有11～14分钟的时间让大家展示自己的语言水平，有些慢热的同学刚走进考场的时候舌头就打结，直到考试快结束时才慢慢进入状态，一切都晚了！所以，考前大家可以拿起最新的口语考题，然后轻松地朗读一下Part 1和Part 3的题目。这样可以帮助大家的舌头和口腔时刻保持活动，到考试时就不需要花时间热身啦！

练习2：临考总结，理清思路

考前除了保持一定的语感练习之外，还要让自己的头脑冷静下来。回头总结一下自己的问题以及考试时自己需要注意的事项还是很有必要的。可以从以下几个方面总结：

- 自己还有哪些发音是经常犯错的？
- 语法上的一些低级小错误是否都注意到了？
- 当自己需要思考时，能否自然地使用语气补白？
- 当自己紧张忘记了某个单词时，是否能迅速避难就易？
- 自己会不会在紧张关头语速时快时慢？
- 自己的非语言因素是否都注意到了呢？

3. 蹲点预测，有备而战

如果考生在考前能大体知道有哪些重点题目，做到有备而战，对于考生临场发挥会有很大帮助。现在有极少数同学被安排在星期五提前考口试，大部分同学都是星期六或星期天甚至是星期一考口试。越往后考试的考生题目越有可能是前面考过的旧题，所以大家可以在周五开始就去到考场或者在网上蹲点以收集各地的当天考题了。去到考场蹲点实在是很麻烦的一件事，同学们可以在网上看"烤鸭"们的当天考后回忆，这样既省事又安全。

网上很多老师会在考前贴出一些口语考试预测和蹲点回忆，同学们可以用以参考。我也会在每次考前收集全国各地的考题，编辑成"早D蹲点报告"贴在博客http://joedy7.blog.163.com里，大家考前上去看看吧，希望对大家有帮助。

4. 悉心打扮，全力以赴

美国心理学家奥伯特·麦拉比指出，人与人在社交过程中，会对彼此留下总体的印象，而社交印象的形成主要取决于：

※55%外表

这里外表指的是考生的着装，个人面貌与精神面貌等。雅思口语考试是考生与考官一对一面对面的考试，考官毕竟是一个有主观思想有感情的人，考生对自己的服装和外观适当进行修饰，能使自己在口试中给考官留下一个美好的印象。当然，考生也不需要过分讲究自己的服饰与仪容，需遵循的原则就是"不必过于刻意，也不宜过于随意"，自然的能体现个人风格的装扮就最好了。另外，头发要整齐干净的，不要给人邋邋遢遢的感觉。

※38%谈吐

一个人的谈吐包括语气，语调，嗓音，手势，表情。

当然，考生除了适当的装扮，还需要体面的举止，考生的态度要显得自然、亲切和积极。会心而真诚的微笑，是无声的语言，是交流中的润滑剂，也是给自己加油鼓劲的心理暗示，能让考生与考官的沟通更加顺利。另外，适当的眼神交流也是必要的，能显示考生对考官的尊重。最后，记得不要急着抢答考官的问题或者把考试变成辩论。先耐心让考官问完整个问题，然后给自己几秒钟时间思考清楚后才从容作答。当发现考官与自己的意见有点不同的时候，不必急于为自己辩驳，镇定自若地陈述自己的观点会让考官感觉到与你交流的诚意。

※7%谈话内容

看，交谈对方一般只有7%的时间在关注考生在讲什么呢。

举个简单的例子，一模一样的一份演讲稿，让两个不同的演讲者来演绎，会得出截然不同的效果。成功的演讲者会随着不同的内容改变自己的语调以及作出不同的手势与表情，从而让听者不断地被演讲的内容所吸引；而不善于演讲与交流的人永远只会用同一类腔调、同一个表情和同一种姿势，这样只会让听众感到无趣，就算演讲的内容再精彩也无济于事。

所以，考生大可不必担心自己的答案是否完美是否标准，大胆积极地说吧！

第 **3** 章

点评

雅思口语最新真题

好了，啰嗦了那么久，大家对雅思的整体考试形式以及要求有了总体的了解了吧？尽管在前面给大家归纳了雅思口语考试三部分的解题技巧，但是在真正的考试过程中，肯定会遇到这样或那样的状况。也就是说真正实战过程中，还有很多小细节是需要注意的。所以从本章开始，正式进入实战阶段！在接下来的八节真题点评里，会按照不同的话题挑选今年最新的考题和大家一起来探讨雅思真题的回答的模式和技巧，还会给大家提供一定的参考词汇、句式以及背景材料。

大家一起来努力攻克雅思口语吧！

第 *1* 节　Personal Information

Greeting and introduction

考试刚开始的时候，考官在确认了考生没有带手机或者手机已经关闭的情况下，开始对考生的身份进行确认，通常考官会用以下的开场白：

Good morning/afternoon.

Can you tell me your full name, please?

What shall I call you?

Can you tell me where you are from?

May I see your ID card, please?

这个时候其实考试还没有开始，考生在这个阶段的回答宜简洁不宜啰嗦，直接答一句话就OK啦！下面会具体给大家示范如何回答这几个开场白问题的。

Lesson 1 听题训练

在还没正式讲解真题之前，要提醒大家注意：Part 1的问题尽管是跟考生熟悉的话题息息相关，但是正是因为考生自认为很熟悉，很容易就掉以轻心不好好复习准备了。到真正考试时有很多同学都容易思维定式导致出现走题的情况，例如有一次当考官问到一个同学What is your favorite weather?的时候，那个同学想都没想就回答It is Summer. 显然他是把"季节"和"天气"两个概念混淆在一起了；还有一次考官问到How many meals do you have every day?时，很多同学都回答I have two cups of milk every day. 很明显大家的思维定式很严重，把meal当成milk了。像这样的例子还有很多，这个时候考官心里肯定会想：这个学生到底是听力的问题还是口语的问题？所以大家先来好好练习一下听题的准确性吧。

★复述练习

现在来做一个pair work的练习，让你的partner为你按正常语速读出以下Part 1的常见考题，然后你迅速地复述出你partner刚刚念出的问题。这个复述刚开始时可以是完全的照搬，像听写一样。但是慢慢地大家就可以只听到几个关键词就通过自己的理解用自己的语言把问题复述出来了。这个过程能很好地锻炼大家准确听题的能力，试试看吧！

Name
● May I have your full name, please?
● What can I call you?
● Does your name have any special meaning?
● Is your name popular in China?
● What kinds of names are popular in China?
● What special habits do Chinese have when giving names to a baby?

Hometown
● Where do you come from?
● What is famous / special about your hometown?
● Do you enjoy living there?
● What do you like most about your hometown?
● Are there any interesting places to see in your hometown?
● What would you say about the people in your hometown?
● Are there any changes in the past few years?
● What do you think needs improvement in your hometown?
● Where else would you like to live if you had the chance? Why?

Studies
● Do you work or are you a student?
● What is / was your major?
● Why did you choose it as your major?
● What do you like about your school?
● Do you like to study alone or in a group?
● How is your relationship with your classmates?
● What do you think of your teachers?
● Are teachers strict with students at your school?

Job
● What is your job?
● How long have you been doing this job?
● What are your main responsibilities at work?
● Do you find your job interesting?
● What is the most difficult part of your job?
● Do you like working alone or in a team? Is teamwork beneficial?
● Are you going to change your job?
● Would you recommend your job to others? Why?

Lesson 2 真题点评与参考答案

Name

● **May I have your full name, please?**

Alright. My name is Li Ming（李明）.

✓Joedy点评：

这里是刚开始考官检查考生身份时间的常规问题，考生不需要按照英语习惯说成Ming Li，按照自己身份证上的顺序简单回答就可以啦。

另外，很多同学在听到full这个单词时，总是反应不过来。因为，考生当中很多人平时都把full读错了，正确的发音应该是短音，也就是 [ful]。

大家千万不要把它读成fool [fu:l]，我们可不是笨蛋啊！

● **What can I call you?**

You can just call me Sam.

✓Joedy点评：

考官在这里不一定是要问考生的英文名字，如果考生没有英文名字，可以大方表示：I am afraid I have no English name, but all my friends call me Xiao Ming, so you can call me that if you like.

● **Does your name have any special meaning?**

Yes, I think so. My parents told me that Xu in my name means the sun and Hui means brightness. I guess they gave me this name hoping that I can have a bright future.

✓Joedy点评：

这里说的name通常指的是考生的given name，也就是姓名里面的"名"，考生不必逐字解释，挑选一个最突出的解释一下就OK了。

和世界上其他父母一样，中国父母也很重视名字，通常父母都会在大家的名字上寄予无限的期望，例如大家的名字一般都包含以下的意义：

① strength and firmness （e.g. 强、柏、龙）

② beauty （e.g. 美、娇、俊）

③ health （e.g. 康、健）

④ intelligence （e.g. 聪、颖、明）

⑤ elegance （e.g. 雅、文、君）

⑥ success （e.g. 辉、豪、翔）

⑦ wealth （e.g. 伟、宏、建）

⑧ luck and happiness （e.g. 祥、怡）

● Is your name popular in China?

No, I don't think so. So far, I haven't met anyone whose name is exactly the same as mine.

✓Joedy点评：

这类问题要求考生回答一个客观的现状，只需先直接作答(yes / no)，然后用detailed information作为补充说明即可。

● What kinds of names are popular in China?

I think names which mean handsomeness are very popular among males such as "Jun" while those names which mean happiness like "Xin" are very common for females. Many of my friends are given these two names.

✓Joedy点评：

Part 1的问题都是围绕着考生的个人信息方面展开的，在回答的时候从自己的角度如实作答就OK，不必一定要追求标准答案。

如上题，那位同学通过自己的观察，以偏概全地总结出"俊"与"欣"是最常见的名字，并且用自己身边的朋友作为证明。这个答案不一定每个人都赞同，但是这些个性化真诚的答案才是考官最喜欢的。同学们多点从自身出发去思考问题吧，不必凡事都追求标准答案的！

● What special habits do Chinese have when giving names to a baby?

As far as I know, a lot of Chinese parents still believe that the given names can influence the children's fate and future. So they always find good characters to name their children. Some people even go to ask for help from fortune tellers.

✓ Joedy点评:

以下是从http://www.foreignercn.com上摘录下来的一小段描述，大家可以看看作为
参考。

Like the western countries, the surnames were symbol of the family and they were handed down from ancestors. But given names can be taken as indications of the parents' hope for their children.

The characters such as "Wen" (文means intelligence), "Wu" (武means martial), "Ming" (明means brightness), "Jie" (杰means outstanding), "Long" (龙means dragon), "Hu" (虎means tiger), "Xin" (信means faith), "Zhi" (智means wisdom), "Yi" (义means justice) and "Li" (礼means courtesy) were always used in given names for boys.

For Girls characters like "Lan" (兰means orchid), "Fang" (芳means fragrance), "Zhu" (珠means pearl), "Ya" (雅means elegance), "Xiu" (秀means beautiful), "Ling" (灵means clever), "Hua"(华means glory), "Hong" (红means red), "Zhen" (贞means chastity), "Shu"(淑means gentle), "Jing" (静means quiet) were widely used.

Hometown

● **Where do you come from?**

I come from Guangzhou and I have been living there since I was born. For me, Guangzhou is a nice place to live in though it is a bit crowded.

✓ Joedy点评:

这个问题可以说是Part 1最没有创意的问题了，几乎每个同学都会被考官问到。但是考生回答的时候依然要做到"态度积极"，用Part 1的回答模式：general information + detailed information的模式来回答就最好了。如参考答案中，该考生先说了I am from Guangzhou作为直接回答，然后补充了具体的信息，如how long I have been living here and what I think about my hometown。这样的回答才显得既积极又自然。

● **What is famous / special about your hometown?**

Well, I guess Guangzhou is famous for its food and people who really like eating at restaurants. Tourists visiting Guangzhou can find various snack bars almost everywhere and the local food will always make their mouth water.

✓ Joedy点评:

一般讲到家乡，很多同学都会习惯性滥用两个词：beautiful, friendly，考官一定就想打瞌睡了。在跟人交流时，最忌讳的就是泛泛而谈，显得毫无诚意。所以大家要养成说话要具体不要空泛的习惯，不需要强求全方位都谈到，只需在一点展开就OK啦！

如关于家乡的信息，考生可以展开的一般有：

	seaside	海滨	mountains	山
1. scenery	lake	湖	forest	森林
	river	江河	grasslands	草原
	soup	汤水	noodle	面条
2. food	meat	肉食	vegetable	蔬菜
	light	清淡的	heavy	难消化的
	spicy	多香料的	hot	辣的
	humid	潮湿	dry	干燥
3. climate	It's like spring all the year round. 四季如春。			
	My hometown has four clearly distinctive seasons. 我家乡四季分明。			

其实谈论家乡不需要谈论得过于深入，大家大可不必辛辛苦苦去查阅大量关于家乡的一些名人或者名胜古迹，那些词既难记又拗口，何必呢？

● **Do you enjoy living there?**

Yes, I do enjoy living in Guangzhou because I have lived here all my life and I have got used to the life here. Besides, I have so many friends here.

● **What do you like most about your hometown?**

I can sum up the greatest feature of Guangzhou in one word, which is 'dynamic'. There are so many interesting places to see and unlimited chances to eat good food here.

● **Are there any interesting places to see in your hometown?**

Yes, there are. Changlong Happy World is one of the very interesting places for people to relax. Its amazing amusement equipment can help the visitors experience excitement, enjoy happiness and relax body and mind.

✓ **Joedy点评：**

其实广州好玩的地方还有不少，我从http://www.701sou.com搜到了以下的介绍，希望对大家有参考作用。

※Changlong Happy World 长隆欢乐世界

Changlong Happy World, planned and designed by the world famous theme park design organization Canada Forrec Company, adopts European style design and has pioneered the domestic European amusement park mode. Most domestic amusement parks pay much attention to theme packaging but neglect amusement equipment, Changlong Happy World pays much attention to amusement equipment and natural eco environment. Changlong Happy World uses the international first class and the most advanced amusement equipment, combining the original natural and ecological features in Changlong to make the visitors experience excitement, enjoy happiness and relax body and mind in a beautiful natural ecological environment.

※Big Hippo Water World 大河马水上世界

Big Hippo Water World located in Nanhu National Tourism and Holiday Zone is the largest, the most fancy, the best and the first water world with international standards in China. There are many exciting and best water facilities including Breakers Bay, down stream, surfing yacht, kids' wading pool, standard swimming pool and drifting river and convenient and well-equipped supporting facilities as supermarket, restaurant

and relaxing booth. In hot summer, it can take cool and pleasant greeting to you. We believe, everything here will bring you a brand new and pleasant experience.

※Children's Park In Guangzhou 广州儿童公园

Children's Park In Guangzhou with a land area of 11, 000 sq.m. is located at the junction of Renmin Nan Lu and Yide Road, opened for business on January 1, 2006. New Children's Park based on its theme design is for the children below 12 years old. Considering their psychological features, the whole park is decorated with natural plants and insects, and even the tickets are printed with small bees. New Children's Park maintains the high greening coverage rate of the old one, up to 90% and above, and most trees are with big crowns. Banyan trees and love trees characterized the features of Lingnan are used to increase greening coverage rate. The old and famous trees in the old Park were all moved to the new one.

● **What would you say about the people in your hometown?**

I think people in my hometown are quite down-to-earth and business-oriented. I think it is this practical spirit that makes Guangzhou develop very fast.

● **Are there any changes in the past few years?**

Yes. I can see the tremendous changes in the past few years especially Guangzhou's development to the east. For example, the Tianhe Area which was quite remote a few years ago is now seen lots of extensive high-rises and a dramatic skyline.

✓Joedy点评：

以下是来源于http://www.guangzhou.gov.cn中一个外国人Herr Detlef Boldt眼中广州的变化，很有趣，供大家参考。

Guangzhou in my eyes

—By Herr Detlef Boldt, Consul-General of Germany to Guangzhou

Nearly half a year, I have been very glad to take Guangzhou as my new home. I am very surprised to this.

Several months ago, I was living in New York which is called the center of the world. I didn't know anything about the place I would live in for several years called Guangzhou. So I didn't know many advantages of Guangzhou. On the map published in the western world, the city is named Kanton. I heard that it was a place crowed with factories and full of dust. And the dishes were very special. So I didn't have much hope to it.

When I arrived at the Baiyun Airport, my imaginary Guangzhou was approved: an old airport, an old and low waiting building, no world famous airplanes on the ground, but the unknown Chinese airplanes. When the airplane I got on from Beijing to Guangzhou stopped on the ground, I had to get off the airplane, in an old manner, stepping down through a ladder I felt very out-of-date. The only pleasant thing is that it was a sunny day, and a clerk from Guangdong Foreign Affairs Office came to the dragging way waiting for me, and expressed a warmly welcome to me.

My feeling was getting better on the way from the airport to the downtown. I found that Guangzhou has as many high buildings as New York does. They are exactly as good as those in New York.

Now I have been living in Guangzhou for five months, and I have been being very glad all the time. Soon, I learned that Guangzhou is a metropolis full of energies, with a great number of historical ancient remains, old city district co-existing with modern and full of traditional tone, modern public basic facilities, parks, museums, musical halls, modern sports buildings, exhibition halls, luxurious hotels, etc. Guangzhou has a general basic facilities and a modernization industry.

Obviously, these achievements have been made all in the last 20 years. Yet, it still keeps fast developing day by day. Cranes seen everywhere in the central districts is telling that: The ancient Guangzhou is disappearing continuously. Today's Guangzhou is a modern metropolis. Tomorrow's Guangzhou will be an ultra-modern metropolis with modern airport, modern harbor, and modern communications. In one word, Guangzhou will be a proud city of China.

Guangzhou people like to present with foreigners. My wife and I have been asked many times to be taken photos with the citizens in the streets. Guangzhou people are working hard, the whole city full of an atmosphere of action. All the people know that they are better than before, and they also know that they will absolutely have a hope for a much better future than today.

In Guangzhou, people not only work happily but also enjoy their lives as much as they like. Guangzhou is still a city full of creation. I feel very happy living in Guangzhou. I once had a badge painted with "I love New York". If anyone in Guangzhou who makes a badge painted "I love Guangzhou", I will certainly buy it and keep it on my chest.

● **What do you think needs improvement in your hometown?**

Air pollution and other forms of environmental degradation are undeniably in existence in big cities like Guangzhou despite the amazing rate of economic development.

● **Where else would you like to live if you had the chance? Why?**

I would choose to live in Australia or just some place with a lot of nature and fewer buildings. The city I am living in is always noisy and I am quite fed up with it now.

Studies

● Do you work or are you a student?

Presently I am a student. I have been studying at Zhongshan University for two years. I will graduate in two years.

● What is / was your major?

I am studying chemistry and it is really interesting.

● Why did you choose it as your major?

Chemistry is really cool because I can experiment on different kinds of chemicals to see what different things they do when mixed together.

✓Joedy点评：

下面来看看国外网友对于他们所选择的不同的专业的看法。

I'm a guy like the outdoors, like driving around, working on stuff with my hands. Not so into staring at a computer all day but will do it if the money's right. That's why I choose **Mechanical Engineering**.

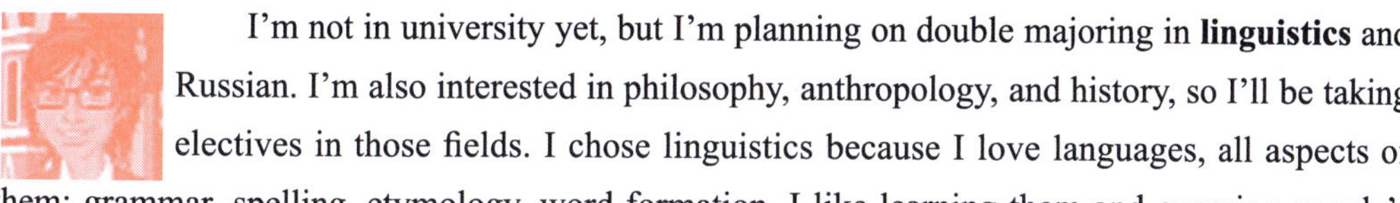

I'm not in university yet, but I'm planning on double majoring in **linguistics** and Russian. I'm also interested in philosophy, anthropology, and history, so I'll be taking electives in those fields. I chose linguistics because I love languages, all aspects of them: grammar, spelling, etymology, word formation. I like learning them and guessing people's native language by their accent. These are the sort of traits that made me see linguistics was a good match for me. I decided to take up Russian as well because I love the language, literature, and culture. I'd also like to become fluent in a second language since my ultimate goal is to become a professor of linguistics and I don't want to be a monolingual.

I am doing a double major in **Biology** and **Psychology**, with a minor in **Sociology**. I choose Psychology major because I find psychology fascinating and I would also like to choose Sociology minor because I am good at sociology and it's nice to have all those easy A's. I choose Biology major because I needed another major to graduate with honors and this major at my university is very flexible in terms of course choice.

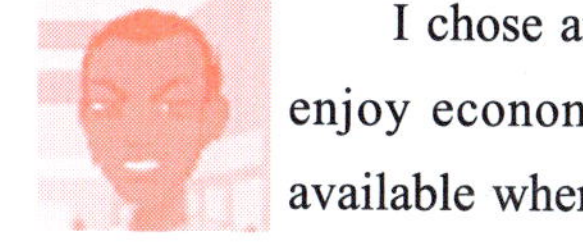

I chose an **economics** major. I love it. I guess it takes 'special people' to really enjoy economics to the extent that I do. I'll have many different opportunities available when I graduate. I love working with numbers and solving problems. I get this immense thrill when I finally discover the value of x... but I need math that is applicable. I need to understand what 'x' is and why it is important.

I'm studying **accounting**. I almost dropped it because everyone told me that it was boring and this and that. I started taking the classes now, and I'm so glad I didn't change it. It might be boring for anyone else — but I love it. I guess majors like mine and yours are the ones that are the best. Because most people will get out of it simply because of what people say or their expectations of it. When in reality they're really good majors and we'll be making a lot of money in the long-run.

I am in **law** school and I chose it because I have always wanted to be a lawyer. I have a love / hate relationship with it. It is difficult and hard, but it is the only way to achieve my dreams... I can not wait until this coming semester when I actually get an internship or paying job... where I get to put my knowledge to work.

✓Joedy 点评：

大家有没有发现呢？国外的学生即使在简单的交流中，也会很明确地表达自己的观点以及适度地围绕自己的观点而扩展补充具体信息。成功的交流就应该是这样的，态度积极很重要啊！

● **What do you like about your school?**

There are a variety of activities held annually in my school and I enjoy them because my social skills can be improved.

✓Joedy 提示：

下面是摘自http://news.bbc.co.uk的学生讨论，大家看看。

"I like school because I get to do things that I can't do at home and I love seeing my **friends**." My school is small so everyone knows each other.

—Adelaide, Amsterdam

"I love my school because the **teaching staff** and our **facilities** are good, our **standard of learning** is excellent and our **success rate** is very high. I am at a specialist languages school so lots of extra languages are available and there are three compulsory languages, so our chances of getting good jobs are good."

—Holly, Kent

"I love my school because I have great friends and the teaching staff are so supportive and encouraging. Every school year we have the opportunity to choose from a list of **holiday activities** and go on them with our school. It's such good fun! This year I'm going on a water sports week."

—Mia, London

"I like my school because we have really friendly staff! They are always there to help if we have any problems and are always fair about things."

—Katie, London

"The best thing about my school would have to be our **school library** because there's internet access on all of the computers and an area where you can just sit and read quietly or do your homework, I love to read."

—Emma, Ferndale

✓Joedy 点评：

大家也许不知道，以上发表意见的都是约10～13岁的学生，他/她们的论述尽管稚嫩，但是绝对不是敷衍了事的！后面的补充说明很重要啊！

● Do you like to study alone or in a group?

I like to study in a group because I won't feel bored and we can help each other through the discussion.

✓Joedy 点评：

大家还可以有不同的回答，大家看看不同的观点吧。

*赞同 studying alone

I find studying alone much better for me because I get distracted really easily, and most of the time, I would rather joke and talk with my friends than study with them. While alone, the focus of study can be easily kept, with little distraction which always accompanies a group of students.

While references are adequate, to study alone is not only possible but it is also helpful to cultivate the ability to solve problems, and furthermore enhance one's independence. Moreover, by keeping focus and developing independence, students become more and more competitive, which is often deemed as a necessary quality.

*赞同 studying in a group

When learning with a group, discussing and debating become possible, which usually create a perfect environment to develop critical thinking skills, where many problems can even be solved unconsciously. While references are not easily accessible, students' knowledge varies from one to another, they can complement each other, and therefore save much time and energy.

*视情况而定

As for me, my preference depends on what subject I am learning or the phase in which I am.

Different subjects may bring different choices. For example, if I were practicing piano, I'd better practice alone. If I were doing physical experiments, team work would always be needed. Different phases also make choices different. Suppose I were learning a foreign language. If I were practicing my basic pronunciation, I'd better learn it by myself. For an adult learner, a tape recorder would be fairly adequate. But if I were to practice my spoken skills, to study alone would be a poor choice. I should look for or create an opportunity to learn it with a group, therefore I can learn it more effectively.

大家参考不同的情况选择自己喜欢的回答方式吧！

● How is your relationship with your classmates?

It's good. Our friendships are very firm and we help each other no matter in study or in life.

● What do you think of your teachers?

I like my teachers. They are patient. Whenever we have questions, they will teach us till we understand.

● Are teachers strict with students at your school?

Yes, they are especially in class. But I think it is good for us, because we can concentrate in class.

✓ Joedy 提示：

很多同学都搞不清楚到底strict的具体定义是什么，来看看大家对于strict teachers的看法吧！

A strict teacher must be firm and strict in the rules but he/she must not appear as horror. He / She would stand to principles, not easily giving in to the demands of some students and parents. A perfectionist teacher dislikes any mistake or carelessness on the part of the students.

It depends on what you mean by "strict" — I have a really strict math teacher who will get mad at the smallest thing, but still likes to joke around with our class and talk. Since the class is high level there aren't really many problems regarding discipline. But the more interesting thing is that he is one of the best teachers, his students get higher scores on the test than those of other math teachers do.

Really, unless you have a problem with the following rules, there shouldn't be any worries.

Well, for me I really like teachers who are strict if he is doing it in a right way. I don't like teachers who are lax and have no control of their class. If the teacher is strict, students will behave and once they behave, they will learn faster. If the teacher loses control and has unruly class, no learning would take place.

I think teachers should show his strictness to the naughty students, but show his friendliness to the pacific students. If the teacher always shows the strictness to all his students, then all the students will be afraid of him and they will not get the good grade under his strictness. In my personal point of view, teachers should put their strictness in a proper way. Sometimes they would be flexible to something, but teachers must be firm.

I don't like strict teachers. Students will learn better and more, if they find a teacher who is more like a friend, in fact, they will get more motivated as they are not under any pressure. They will work on their own, not because of the fact that they are afraid. With a strict teacher, they will find it difficult to ask anything, or any doubt, as they are scared. This will result in a communication gap between a teacher and a student.

Job

- What is your job?

I am now working in a medium-size firm as a secretary reporting to the sales director in southern China region.

- How long have you been doing this job?

For almost 3 years. I started just as a sales assistant in a tiny sales team.

- What are your main responsibilities at work?

The most important things in my job are to make clear sales reports monthly or accordingly and make well-arranged daily routines for my boss. Also, I need to coordinate the whole sales force in every big strategy.

✓Joedy 点评：

这个同学的回答很是精彩，有以下三点值得大家学习。

※ 直接地回答问题the most important things in my job are to...，但是没有机械化地重复（echo）考官的问题；

※ 巧妙而灵活地运用连接词突出了前后的逻辑关系，例如or表选择，and表递进，also表补充；

※ 适度扩展，信息很丰富，这是态度非常积极的回答。

● Do you find your job interesting?

I would say that my job is challenging rather than interesting. It needs my 100% patience and carefulness. If I ever I made any tiny mistakes, the whole team would be in incredible trouble.

● What is the most difficult part of your job?

Being aware of everything is the most difficult part. I have to be fast, considerate, careful and show initiative. I also have to be optimistic when my boss is nasty to me.

✓Joedy 点评：

看看不同职业的人对于不同职业的描述吧，各行都有自己的难处啊。

I work at **the front desk of a hotel**. Dealing with angry guests who seem to think everything in this world, including weather and their travel mistakes like forgetting to rent a car, is my fault. Yes, it is my fault that your flight was delayed for two hours in Denver, I should have been waiting with the red carpet to role out for you upon your arrival. I think I deal with stupid people by being so sarcastic, it makes me laugh and relieve my stress.

I'm an **administrative assistant** and the most annoying thing is having to answer everyone's phone calls when the caller doesn't dial an extension. Most of these calls are angry clients screaming at me about stuff I know nothing about. All I can do is to send them to the voicemail of the right person if this right person can't speak to them for some reason.

I am a **medical assistant** and I would say dealing with difficult patients is a challenge. You need patience and you need to remember that they can be scared and nervous and take out their anxiety on you. Also, there are some doctors who think they are god and treat you like dirt; others are quick to blame you if something goes wrong. They want to avoid taking responsibility for anything they could get sued over.

I worked in a **library** for several years in college and there was one thing that was very stressful. Dealing with customers! Believe me people want and demand some really outrageous things at times and can be particularly nasty when they are not given what they want. They get really nasty too when they receive fines or other penalties.

● Do you like working alone or in a team? Is teamwork beneficial?

As a secretary, I prefer working alone for the best accuracy; while as a sales coordinator, I do enjoy team work, which can help fasten the whole process of everything.

✓Joedy 点评：

很多同学都问："假如一个问题有两个方面，是否可以说It depends然后就分两方面论述啊？"

其实世界上所有事物都有它的两面性，客观全面地论述的确无可厚非。但是我非常担心的是，很多同学一旦两面都论述，很容易就会迷失方向，论述到最后连自己都不知道自己在讲什么了。特别是口语不同于写作，随意性很强，没办法时刻保持逻辑性。所以同学们如果真的想分开两方面论述的话，记得要时刻保持清醒的头脑。

看看下面的参考，国外的朋友即使论证两面，也是有侧重点的。

I prefer working alone. Some of the people I am working with are either slackers or egotistical jerks who insist on doing everything because no one else is good enough for them.

I prefer to work on a team (assuming my teammates are competent and responsible), because then I can usually have more fun while finishing the job. It would be great if I'm working in a group in which everyone contributes equally.

● Are you going to change your job?

Probably. I would love to have a job in which I can use all my skills. I wish I could be a trainer some day to share my experience with the fresh workmates.

● Would you recommend your job to others? Why?

I am more than willing to because it is really challenging and offers great opportunity for personal improvement and re-evaluation.

第2节　Clothing and Fashion

Clothing是Part 1的常见考题，大家还是要练好听题，避免听不懂问题乱回答。大家大声朗读下面的问题，有不清楚发音的单词记得要查好词典，例如occasion [ə'keiʃən]，自己要会读才能保证听得懂考官的话。朗读的时候最好把自己读出来的句子用MP3录下来，然后回头听自己的录音，看是否听得懂。

Lesson 1 Part 1 听题训练

Clothing and fashion
● What kind of clothes do you like to wear?
● What type of clothing do you wear on different occasions?
● What do you wear when you are working / at school?
● What are the differences in the clothes between now and in the past?
● What kind of clothes do children usually wear?
● What information can you get in another person's clothing?
● Do you like to follow fashion?
● What are the benefits of wearing uniforms?

Lesson 2 Part 1 真题点评与参考答案

Clothing and fashion

● What kind of clothes do you like to wear?

I am personally very into current fashion especially jeans and tops, and I also like mashing different styles together.

● What type of clothing do you wear on different occasions?

I will wear formal clothes in meetings or wedding and fashionable clothes of parties.

✓Joedy 提示：

大家注意，occasion [əˈkeiʒən]这个单词，很多同学都读错或者是听不清考官在讲什么，所以大家要好好读准这个单词。occasion这个单词指的是"场合"，场合一般分两种：formal和informal。大家当然会在不同场合穿不同衣服啦！

那西方国家的人们是不是也是这样的呢？看看吧。

Men	Women
Formal and semiformal	*Formal and semiformal*
tuxedo 宴会礼服 suit 套装，西服 uniform 制服	designer dress 出自名设计师之手的礼服 evening dress 晚礼服
informal	*informal*
T- shirt or shirt with jeans	simple top with jeans

● What do you wear when you are working / at school?

When studying at school, I have to wear a uniform. That's the rule. We don't really like it.

● What are the differences in the clothes between now and in the past?

It changes a lot. In the past, there were fewer choices we could choose from. People wore very simple colors. But now, we have more choice.

● What kind of clothes do children usually wear?

Most children like to wear clothes with cartoon patterns. During school days children are required to wear school uniforms.

● What information can you get in another person's clothing?

Clothing can tell quite a lot about a person. I always believe clean, neat clothes say that the person has both self-respect and respect for other people; they are well organized and disciplined.

✓Joedy 提示：

参考其他同学的看法吧。

Clean, neat clothes say that the person has both self-respect and respect for other people; they are well organized and disciplined. Even the simplest, casual clothes can convey this impression while expensive yet wrinkled outfit will betray your sloppy side. That is also the reason why those in the military are required to wear clean and neat uniforms.

✓Joedy 点评：

这位同学的答案的独特之处在于他运用了对比的手法，指出整洁的衣服和皱皱的衣服给别人留下截然不同的印象，然后给出了军人需要穿整洁制服的例子，不需要大条道理就已经清楚地表明立场。

As for me, style of the clothes that a person wears is a big teller of his / her character, priorities, and social standing (to some extent). Classic style shows a more serious and traditionally-inclined personality while bright, extravagant outfits speak of being non-conventional, or perhaps artistic. Many actors and musicians are known for unusual, flashy clothes meant to draw attention and show their exclusiveness, their being different from the rest.

✓Joedy 点评：

这位同学在最后提出有关明星穿衣风格的例子是答案的画龙点睛之处，再一次证明了用事实说话的力量。来看看另外一个从穿衣风格入手的答案吧。

Someone dressed according to the latest fashion, although this particular style is not very flattering to his or her figure, reveals lack of individuality or personal taste. On the contrary, someone who wears an **impeccable** outfit that perfectly suits them and yet is not the latest trend demonstrates being able to rise above the crowd.

✓Joedy 点评：

大家可能对impeccable这个单词感到陌生，其实也可以换成 faultless, flawless或者是 perfect。

● Do you like to follow fashion?

No, I don't. When I go shopping I look for clothes that are comfortable, and look good on me. If it's in the store it's trendy. But I will wear what I buy for as long as it fits, and is in good condition, even if it goes out of style. I tend to stick to classic styles anyway.

✓Joedy 提示：

是否应该追潮流引起了大家热烈地讨论，正反面的探讨非常有意思，我挑选了比较精彩的论述。大家也来看看，形成自己的独特观点就好。

YES	NO
We've been raised in a society where you can become prominent or powerful only upon the support of others, so logically you follow the trend. You do it for popularity and being considered the normal. One goal everyone has in life is to be accepted and following fashion trends is another way of doing so.	Fashion is created by people who dare to think differently and outside of the box. If you follow your own fashion, you might start a new trend! Also, it's always good to stick to your own beat instead of following others. If people comment on your clothes in a negative way, it's because they aren't brave enough to step outside of the fashion vortex and try something of their own. Go with your own flow.

● What are the benefits of wearing uniforms?

No doubt that wearing uniforms can make people more formal and respectable.

✓Joedy 提示：

关于uniforms的好处，主要是从对于学校，学生个人的角度来思考的。

对于学校管理而言：

A school uniform makes it easier for the school authorities to recognize students belonging to their school. With school uniforms, there is no need for school authorities to police what the students wear. Thus, daily battles regarding what's appropriate or not for school can be avoided.

对于学生个人而言，制服的好处在于：

⭐ A school uniform apparently also saves students from putting their fashion tastes before their learning requirements. More time can be devoted to getting an education when students are spared wasting time wondering what to wear and how to make a fashion statement.

⭐ Wearing the same type of dress reduces social snobbery and peer pressure in educational institutions. It is also supposed to reduce incidents of bullying and theft, which are two main types of juvenile crime on campus. It is not likely that you pick on someone for wearing the same dress as yourself or steal a pair of shoes you both have and can afford.

⭐ A school uniform can instill a sense of discipline as well as a sense of belonging. This naturally reduces incidents of violence. Students can come to school without worrying about personal safety.

✓Joedy 点评：

以上的几个答案的共同之处是着重于问题的一个方面，然后进行适度地展开。记住，口语考试并不需要面面俱到。

Lesson 3 Part 2 审题训练与真题点评

★ Part 2 审题训练

> Describe a piece of clothing you wear on special occasions:
> You should say:
>> When you bought it.
>> Where you bought it.
>> How it looks.
>> How people thought about it.
> And explain the reason why you like wearing it.

✓Joedy 提醒：

这张卡片是让考生描述一件在特定场合穿的衣服，审题的时候一定要注意！那什么场合算是special的呢？其实所谓的special是因人而异的。但是总的来说，special occasions包括了一些celebrations / parties（birthday生日，Christmas party圣诞晚会）；ceremonies（例如adult ceremony成人礼，wedding婚礼，graduation ceremony毕业典礼），还有一些contests啦，当然啦，大家也可以有其他的选择。

大家现在来试着选好题，然后作简单的笔记吧。

★ Part 2真题点评与参考答案

The piece of clothing I would like to wear on special occasion is a shirt. I bought it last summer in the teem plaza. I remember that time I was attracted by the design of the shirt. Compared to other clothes I bought, this shirt is unique actually. First, this is a kind of formal shirt in light purple and white which makes me feel respectable. The most special design is the button. Though the buttons are round like others, there are different patterns on each button. In others words, each button is distinctive and unique. In the back of the shirt, there is a very fantastic logo on it. Very amazing. When I tried it on, my parents also said "it is a very special and wonderful shirt. You should buy it." So now, on some special occasions like wedding, farewell party, I would wear it. I like it.

✓Joedy 提示：

其实每个人喜欢的衣服都是不一样的，讲衣服也不一定要拘泥于讲衣服的"颜色"和"款式"，如果大家对于物品的外观觉得难以描述，就试着去描述一下该物品背后的意义吧，这个时候就是大家讲故事的时候了。例如，考生可以讲这件衣服是某个对自己很重要的人送的，或者是在参加某个对自己非常重要的场合穿的，以突出该衣服对自己的意义。

来看看不同的人有什么不同的看法吧。

My best outfit is everything I wear. I'm such a fashion freak that I try all kinds of different looks to keep the people guessing. My favorite items would have to be my red

LuLu Bay T-shirt, my brown vintage ACDC T-shirt, Diesel Jeans, Express skinny jeans, my gray jumpsuits that I wear during any weather, and my Wet Seal jeans — I wear these all of the time.

All of my clothing is nice. I don't usually go for trendy because it is a huge waste of money. Plus, the dress code at work is stringent to say the least. My shoes, of which I have an Imelda Marcos worthy collection, bring everything together though.

My best pair of jeans and a new black and gold shirt with my knee-high boots are my favorite things to wear. They are comfortable and stylish at the same time.

If you mean dressing up as going to a wedding or something, I have a few skirts and dresses, but I am not fond of wearing skirts and dresses, so I don't make it a habit to have overly nice or expensive ones.

✓Joedy 提示：

大家在生活当中经常会向朋友推荐或者分享一件对自己很重要的物品，特别是女孩子，经常会向朋友推荐一件服饰、一个电子产品、一本书等等。描述物品的话题很多，有没有办法找到其中的关联，以归类准备呢？其实，物品无论千变万化，其背后所存在的意义都是一样的，例如：这件服饰、这个电子产品以及这本书，都可以是收到的一份礼物啊，送这个礼物的人，其对自己的期待以及感情都是一样的，所以，大家只要描述好以下几步就好。

1. What it is like?

2. When and where you use it?

3. How you feel about it?

4. Why it is important to you?

讲到物品背后的意义，无非是对自己成长过程的影响了，大家可以突出这个物品的"教育意义"，例如让自己变得更加睿智wise了，更加自信confident了，更加坚持自己的理想persistent了。大家养成习惯，每天尝试描述一件对自己有意义的物品，然后重点强调其对自己的具体意义所在就好了。

Lesson 4 Part 3 听题训练

Part 3的问题相对Part 1而言难度会加大，词汇的使用也相对会复杂一点。大家更加要保证听懂题目以保证不走题。以下的题目大家都能听得懂吗？是否会有一些词看是看得懂但是读出来的时候模棱两可的呢？如果是这样的话，好好开声去朗读以下的题目并尝试复述出来吧。

Clothes

- What is the difference between clothes now and before?

- What do people in your country wear on formal occasions?

- How has people's clothing style changed these years?

- Why does fashion trend change all the time?

- Why should the staff in shops and companies wear uniforms?

- Do you think uniforms will restrict people's behaviors and kill people's individuality?

Lesson 5 Part 3 真题点评与参考答案

Clothes

What is the difference between clothes now and before?

There is a huge difference. In the past, the design, the style and the material were simple like some traditional clothes my grandparents had. But now, it changes. There are various designs and styles for different people. With the development of technology, material becomes better than before. Some sportswear I wear while I am doing sports is made of nylon. It's comfortable and breathable and water repellent.

What do people in your country wear on formal occasions?

In my country, people usually wear suits in meeting. In my father's room, there are a lot of suits for different kinds of occasions such as the formal suits for significant meetings, the casual suits for small but formal meetings.

How has people's clothing style changed these years?

A few years ago, people dressed almost the same because with underdeveloped technology, the ideas of clothing style could not be easily transmitted in the world. But now, advanced technology makes the communication of different countries frequent. So there are much more clothing styles nowadays.

● Why does fashion trend change all the time?

Because the world is changing all the time and the attitude of people to life, in the world people are changing. So designers will put this new idea in their new design. For example, when wars occur frequently, more design about protecting the world would be made.

● Why should the staff in shops and companies wear uniforms?

In my opinion, wearing uniforms is a sign to demonstrate that they are the staff who respect and serve customers. Sometimes, from the uniforms, we can feel the respect from the staff so we can enjoy shopping more.

✓Joedy 点评：

制服的确是大家一直争论不休的话题。到底穿制服有什么好处呢？为什么大大小小的公司都会有自己的制服文化呢？看看不同国家的人有什么不同看法吧。

Why People Wear Uniforms

Chang-Hong Cheong from Korea

For thousands of years, people have wanted to have a sense of identity apart from others and a strong feeling of belonging to their society. Therefore, people around the world have used things such as flags and uniforms to identify themselves with their societies. Uniforms are one of the most popular ways to do this.

Generally, if students attend schools, schools push them to wear school uniforms. I think they do this for two reasons.

First, students will have to be careful about how they behave when they are wearing uniforms because people can easily identify them and know what school they attend. Second, schools want students to think they belong to the school all the same.

From my experience, government organizations, such as the army or the police, wear special uniforms because they want to stand out from other people. During their military service, all soldiers and officers must wear uniforms to identify themselves.

In my opinion, this is because an army needs to emphasize standardization. Lots of different kinds of people join an army, so it is necessary to unite all these people in order to carry out military goals.

In other words, if an army accepts very different kinds of people, it needs to do this in order to maximize their abilities and achieve common goals. Thus, it requires everyone who joins to wear uniforms.

Hotel Staff Should Wear Uniforms

Agustina Pascual from Spain

I remember the two years I wore a uniform when I worked as a receptionist in a hotel. Our uniform was a suit, a skirt and a jacket. The skirt was grey with a black stripe and the jacket was black.

The hotel had different divisions, and in each one the workers wore different uniforms depending on their positions. For example, the receptionists had more different uniforms than the managers.

I think wearing uniforms has many advantages for staff who wear them. They don't need to buy a lot of elegant clothes or worry about what they wear to work everyday. Also, uniforms are more comfortable for them. Another advantage is that the customers can easily identify them.

● **Do you think uniforms will restrict people's behaviors and kill people's individuality?**

I do think so. The type of clothing people wear expresses themselves. Uniforms keep your uniqueness balled up inside you and you aren't able to show your colors to the world.

✓ **Joedy 点评：**

对于有些人的确认为制服特别是校服极大地限制了学生的个性，大家怎么看待呢？来看看我给大家准备的两个参考答案吧。

答案1. The worst thing of all about wearing school uniforms is that uniforms hinder students' abilities to be unique. While the uniforms may, in fact, hinder certain students from dressing inappropriately, hinder one's abilities to create themselves. Since students may be forced to wear uniforms on certain occasions in the rest of their lives, High School may be one of the few moments when young people have the right to create their own self-image. It is not difficult to imagine how seriously it would be if people have nothing to be different.

答案2. Enforcing an identical dressing code — by this I mean school uniforms — to avoid inappropriate dressing makes no good sense due to the fact that the majority of the student body does not dress inappropriately on a daily basis. There is, undoubtedly, a minor amount of students who do not abide by this rule. If administration took the time to fix the problem individually, there would be no need to punish everyone. Administration would much rather worry about PROM than worry about the student's right to individuality.

✓ **Joedy 点评：**

以上的两个参考答案均具有很强烈的西方特色：崇尚自由，大胆新颖。第一个答案指出制服限制了学生的个性发展，第二个答案则更大胆地认为规定学生穿制服是学校懒惰的行政管理的体现。所以重申一下，雅思口语考试是没有标准答案的，所以尽可能地大胆发挥吧。

第*3*节　Food and Cooking

Lesson 1 Part 1 听题训练

　　"食品"这个单元倒没有太多的难词，但是大家还是要一如既往好好开声读出以下的问题，每天开声的朗读能保持良好语感，把耳朵叫醒吧！

Food and Cooking
● What kind of food do you like? Why?
● Has your taste of food changed much since you were a child?
● Did you learn to cook when you were a child?
● Do children nowadays like cooking?
● Is it necessary to offer cooking lessons at school?
● Is learning cooking necessary for everyone? Why?
● Who does the cooking in your family?
● Who cooks the best in your family?
● How often do you eat out?
● What sorts of restaurants do you like going to?
● Do people often eat out in your hometown or do they cook at home?

Lesson 2 Part 1 真题点评与参考答案

Food and cooking

● What kind of food do you like? Why?

I like spicy food best because it's so delicious and can make me eat more, especially in winter.

● Has your taste of food changed much since you were a child?

Yes, of course. Take spicy food as an example. I started to like it when I was in university. I seldom ate it before then.

● Did you learn to cook when you were a child?

Yes. I had to learn cooking when I was seven because my father thought it was a good way to foster a good personality.

● Do children nowadays like cooking?

Well, I don't think so because I seldom find children enjoy doing housework like mopping, let alone cooking.

● Is it necessary to offer cooking lessons at school?

In my opinion, the schools should offer not only cooking lessons but also lessons on every kind of housework. For it is quite important for them to learn to be independent.

✓Joedy 点评：

现在满大街都是各种各样的restaurant，里面会供应来自不同地区的美味食品，人们根本不需要辛辛苦苦跑去菜市场挑选食材，然后花1～2小时在厨房里忙碌，就可以舒舒服服地享受着美味食品。那人们到底是否还需要学习cooking呢？对children而言，学习cooking还有必要吗？

看看http://betterkidcare.psu.edu这里的专家怎么说。

Eight Great Reasons to Cook with Children

Cooking can give children a great sense of satisfaction. When children cook, they are learning many skills, including math and reading skills as well as how to work together. They also get a chance to practice motor skills through things like pouring, stirring, and measuring. Cooking is a great sensory experience that children enjoy. When you prepare by having the basic supplies on hand and selecting some simple recipes, you are setting the stage for learning and fun through cooking.

Children who have fun cooking with adults learn healthy eating tips, and are doing something active (instead of watching television) and spending quality time with the family. These kids will have a sense of pride when the family sit down to eat the food they created.

Cooking can give children a deep sense of satisfaction and build their self-confidence. It can help them grow in the following ways:

1. Learn about nutrition and increase their willingness to try a new food.

2. Develop valuable self-help skills and increase independence.

3. Develop math concepts through counting, measuring, timing, and ordering events.

4. Work cooperatively with others.

5. Learn to follow directions and complete all the steps necessary to finish a task.

6. Learn science concepts: temperature, volume, how something can change when it is heated, etc.

7. Improve fine motor control through using hand muscles.

8. Express themselves creatively.

● Is learning cooking necessary for everyone? Why?

I don't think it necessary for everyone until he / she needs to cook by themselves. As we know, it's very easy to find something to eat nowadays.

✓Joedy 点评：

当然啦，大家也可以从相反方面去回答。可以说cooking挺重要的！

Of course it is, because learning cooking is one of the most important life skills for those who need to live by themselves.

看，雅思口语考试永远也没有标准答案，答案本身也没有正确与错误之分，从自身角度出发去思考，相信第一感觉，然后自圆其说就可以了。

来看看大家怎么说。

I like the creativity of it and I also like knowing what is in my dinner. When younger, it gave me a sense of independence and when older, it gave me a career.

It's fun, and as others have said, it lets me express my creative side. Cooking lets me indulge once in a while, if I'm only cooking for myself. If I'm cooking for someone else, it allows me to share a part of myself, and gives me a chance to please my friend(s).

People like to cook as they can show a creative side. Also people cook to get away from the world and to relax. To many people cooking is a hobby.

● **Who does the cooking in your family?**

My mother of course. But sometimes my father and I will give her a hand on some big days.

● **Who cooks the best in your family?**

Actually, my father cooks the best since he's a chef. But he wouldn't even enter the kitchen at home because he doesn't want to cook all the time.

● **How often do you eat out?**

It really depends. When my friends ask me or on some important days, I would really like to eat out.

● **What sorts of restaurants do you like going to?**

Special ones of course. Guangzhou is called the heaven of cuisine and there are lots of choices. I especially like eating in special restaurants like Italian and Thai ones.

● **Do people often eat out in your hometown or do they cook at home?**

In my hometown, most people would like to cook at home since they don't have much spare money to eat out.

✓Joedy 点评：

这是一道很典型的客观信息题，大家在扩展答案的时候可以有两个方向：解释原因或

者是具体提供例子。范例里的答案是用了解释原因这个方式去扩展的，现在再看看home-cooked meals还有没有其他benefits。

Health reasons for eating at home

If you're looking for an easy way to delight in a healthy life for you and your loved ones, one of the most effective ways is to prepare home-cooked meals.

With our time being at a premium, preparing your own meals is often replaced with on the go meals at fast food or casual dining establishments. Not only are these choices usually more costly than eating at home, but also not figure friendly. You can drastically increase the health benefits by preparing home-cooked meals.

Eating at Home Gives You the Choice

Eating at home has many health benefits, but most importantly it gives you the choice of what ingredients you decide to cook with or not included in your meals. Have you ever glanced at what a burger at a fast food restaurant is made with — there can be dozens of ingredients, some with names you haven't heard of or cannot pronounce. When you prepare home-cooked meals, you can keep your foods natural and whole.

Do You Have Special Dietary Needs?

Another health benefit of eating at home is that if you have special dietary restrictions such as limitations on sugar in your foods, you can conveniently fix dinners that fit your health needs. No need to fret if the restaurant has a low salt dish or if there is any extra sugar included in a dish.

Portion Control

One of the reasons that many people have gained weight is due to the portions that many casual dining restaurants give you. They are much larger than necessary. If you eat in, you can create the appropriate amounts for you and your loved ones, eliminating unnecessary food intake.

Food Allergies

When you eat at home, you can be more deliberate in preparing foods, especially if you or a family member has a food allergy. Food allergies in many situations can be serious and possibly even fatal. Preparing food at home reduces the risk of an allergic reaction to allergic food.

Quality Time

Another benefit to dining in is the quality time spent together. We all like to be taken care of at times so it's okay to eat out for special events. However, preparing home-cooked meals allows you to spend valued time with family. Everyone can take part in meal preparation so it's a shared event. By allowing children to participate in meal planning and cooking you are teaching them valuable self-sufficiency skills. The ambiance is more conducive to talking.

Make a pledge to prepare more home-cooked meals. The benefits of eating at home exceed the time it takes to prepare a home-cooked meal. Your loved ones will thank you in the end.

Lesson 3 Part 2 审题训练与真题讲解

★ Cue card I 审题训练

> Describe your favorite restaurant / café.
>
> You should say:
>
> Where it is.
>
> How you got to know it.
>
> What is special about it.
>
> And explain why you like going there.

✓ Joedy 提醒：

很多同学都觉得restaurant / café好难讲，大家都认为一讲restaurant就要讲菜式或者烹饪方式，那些单词一定会很难。其实，讲restaurant不一定非得要去讲菜式或者烹饪方式。一间restaurant吸引人们的往往不仅仅是菜式而已，还有其他因素啊。例如，餐馆的环境，特色服务，老板之类的。大家要学会去避开自己不擅长不熟悉的方面，选择自己容易讲的并且熟悉的方面，那这个restaurant就不会是难题啦。

来打个简单的草稿试试吧。

★ Cue card I 真题点评与参考答案

The restaurant I like to go is called Xiang Cun Guan, which means "restaurant in the countryside" in English. It mainly offers Hu Nan cuisine, which is very delicious and spicy. I got to know it because it is just two blocks away

from my home. And there was a big promotion on the day of its opening, so I became a loyal customer since then. The food sold there is not only very typical Hu Nan food but it is also not very expensive, for a meal for four people, around RMB120 can make everyone full. So there is always a long queue outside around dinner time every day. I enjoy going there not only because it is very close to where I live, it is also because I am crazy about Hu Nan cuisine, which is the selling point there. Another point is that it has become a good place for the gathering with my friends. We usually eat out there with a group of crazy people.

★ Cue card II审题训练

Describe a person who is good at cooking.

You should say:

 Who he / she is.

 How he/she learned cooking.

 What his/her best dish is.

 What you can learn from him / her.

And explain why you think he / she is a good cook.

✓Joedy 提醒:

  同样的道理，讲一个cooking很厉害的人，也不一定要讲这个人做什么菜，那道菜具体是如何的好。大家凡是讲人物类的卡片，最好就是用"情"字去打动考官，讲讲这个人对自己产生的影响，讲讲这个人与自己的联系，从侧面去烘托一个人，比直接去死板地描述来得更有效。试试吧，现在打一个简单的草稿吧。

★ Cue card II真题点评与参考答案

  The person who is good at cooking is my father, a chef. He started learning cooking from my grandfather probably when he was 7 years old. As the eldest son, he needed to take care of his brother and sisters as soon as he went to primary school. He was always willing to

share how clumsy he was when cooking. His best dish is grilled lobster with cheese, the most famous dish also in the restaurant he works in. It is not very greasy but very fresh in taste. My father cooks not only for delicious food, but also cooks for the customers' emotion, he hopes that everyone would feel happy when eating his dishes. Besides, he takes care of the family so well that the whole family would feel hard to imagine the life without my father's enthusiasm. That's what I can learn from him and why I think he is the best cook I have ever met.

✓Joedy 点评：

看到了吧，范文里讲父亲是个很好的cook，但是并没有花大量笔墨在描述菜式上面，反而是用最平淡最好懂的语言去表达感情，这样的描述才是最能打动人的。

看看下面摘自http://www.washingtonpost.com关于father平淡又感人的描述吧。

My Dad's Best Cook

Salena Hess says that her dad can really cook — not just some things, but everything. He tries new dishes, tackles complicated recipes and makes delicious sandwiches out of leftovers. The 11-year-old from Arlington says, "My dad's cooking is an amazing thing in my life."

Adam Hess, the weekend chef at the Hesses', is one of many fathers who have cooking duties at home. Around the Washington area, dads are grilling, baking and experimenting. They're cooking for pleasure, to carry on traditions, to feed their families well and to pass on their love of good food. So their kids want us to know this about them:

Venkat Iyer, a 12-year-old from Herndon, never knows what he'll find in his lunchbox. Creativity is the name of the game when his father, Arun Iyer, does the cooking. For Venkat, a typical brown-bag school lunch might contain fresh tomato and mozzarella slices sandwiched between pesto-slathered slices of toasting bread.

Nathan Clukey takes his daughter Abby, 7, into their Falls Church backyard to gather ingredients for their "secret sauce". Then they head back to the kitchen to create the sauce together.

Stay-at-home dad Stavros Cologer packs a lot of cooking into his schedule in his Annapolis home. His kids, 7-year-old Themi and 10-year-old Sophia, rave about his mashed potatoes, cinnamon butter apples and just about everything else he prepares.

The list goes on. When we asked kids to write to us about their dads, e-mail us what they did: We learned about cooking by instinct and baking from recipes, about dads who can make anything and those who have specialties. We met some dads who have perfected just one dish, but what a dish!

Lesson 4 Part 3 听题训练

✓Joedy 提醒：

Part 3的题目相对比较难，Part 3的问题虽然听起来有点复杂，但是都是往一个重点问的。例如restaurant和cooking这两个卡片在Part 3的重点就是问"食品卫生"和"健康饮食"，大家根据问题的重点，平时多加收集观点和论据就OK了！

如果真的是在考试时听不清Part 3的题目，大家可以使用Guess + Confirm的方法，也就是根据重点先猜测一下，然后再去向考官确认就好了。猜错了怎么办？不要紧，考官毕竟是个人啊，人都有"好为人师"的心态，如果我们猜错了，考官一般会帮我们纠正的。大家可以试一下。

下面我们来开声读以下的Part 3的问题，注意保证自己要读对里面的单词，不然考官读出来我们是听不懂的。

Healthy food and food safety

- Are there different types of food in different places in China?

- How do you feel about fast food restaurants?

- How has modern technology changed our diet?

- Do Chinese people like eating healthy food?

- Do you care about how your food is made when you eat at a restaurant?

- Do people in China place much importance on food safety?

- How can the government supervise food safety?

Cooking

- Is it important to have meals with the whole family?
- Do Chinese people often eat at home?
- Why do people cook less now and what are the disadvantages of it?
- How do you get the information of food quality when you are shopping for food?
- Do students like cooking by themselves?
- Is it necessary for students to learn to cook?
- Do children have any idea about junk food?
- Do boys have to be a good cook and what about girls?
- How do students learn to cook?
- Do you think schools should provide cooking lessons?
- Who should be responsible for teaching children to cook, teachers or parents?
- Do schools have the responsibility to provide nutritious food for students?

Healthy food and food safety

● Are there different types of food in different places in China?

Sure! The famous Eight Cuisines in China can even attract people from the farthest corner of the world. In Guangdong Province only, there are two famous ones: Cantonese Food and Chao Zhou Food.

✓Joedy 点评：

这里考生不需要真的细细地把各个地方的菜系都数出来，只要笼统地简单介绍一两个自己很熟悉的就OK了，记住：Say what you can say!

看看下面搜集的信息：

China is a country with a vast territory and many nationalities. Hence, a variety of Chinese food with distinctive but mouthwatering flavor can be found. Generally, it is widely accepted that Chinese food can be roughly divided into eight regional cuisines based on their typical characteristics.

Liaoning and Jilin provinces are places where you can sample dog meat. You can find restaurants of various kinds where you can eat dog meat all over Shenyang, the capital city of Liaoning province. it is said that dog meat used to be very popular in Taiwan.

Cuisine in Guangdong province is more than different types of savory dishes, as is commonly known by people. It is said that people in Guangdong eat the strangest animals, such as snakes and grasshoppers, and this is widely considered as the reason for the outbreak of SARS.

Western China's Xinjiang province is a good destination for Central Asian style food. You do not even need to do the entire Silk Road for tasting the food, because you can find many folks from Xinjiang province on the streets of China's eastern cities cooking and selling cheap kebabs.

I've never heard of crushed beak powder. I'd file that one in with the legendary monkey brains rumor. I haven't yet seen that in even the most remote areas of China.

● How do you feel about fast food restaurants?

Well, many people claim that the food is not nutritious enough but I personally like it because as a member of the OT group, for people who usually have to work over-time, fast food can save us a lot of time in deed.

● **How has modern technology changed our diet?**

Well, one important thing is that there is more and more fast food and packed food appearing in our life, making our diet more and more convenient. But the food is not as fresh as it used to be.

✓ **Joedy 点评：**

2008年闹得沸沸扬扬的"三鹿奶粉"事件，让"食品安全"成为了热门话题。雅思口语考试一向与社会最新话题紧密联系起来，所以food safety这个概念在2008年底的雅思口语测试中出现得很频繁。无可否认，modern technology已经完全改变了我们的饮食习惯以及食物结构，到底这个改变是利是弊呢？

Our Modern Diet

As we face epidemic numbers of people with obesity, diabetes and cardiovascular disease, many people have started to question the role our modern diet plays in our health. There is no doubt that when you compare what we eat today to what our parents or grandparents ate, the changes are enormous. It is very likely that our grandparents wouldn't recognize many of the foods we take for granted and one wonders what would happen to granddad's serum cholesterol, body weight, and overall health if he were to eat the highly processed fast food that is a major part of most of our diets.

There is a branch of science that feels we should be looking even farther back at our ancestors' diets as a way of gauging the quality of our own diet. It is believed that our diet has changed too rapidly and is too far removed from that of our ancient ancestors and this is the cause of many of our modern day nutrition / metabolism / health problems.

Today we eat highly processed food, and not enough fruits and vegetables and our dietary fiber intake is a major concern. It has been only recently (in relative terms) that the amount of fiber in our diets has deceased so rapidly. However, metabolic and physiological changes to accommodate this change in the diet will take much longer. So constipation and perhaps heart disease and some cancers may become major problems because our bodies can't change as fast as our diets.

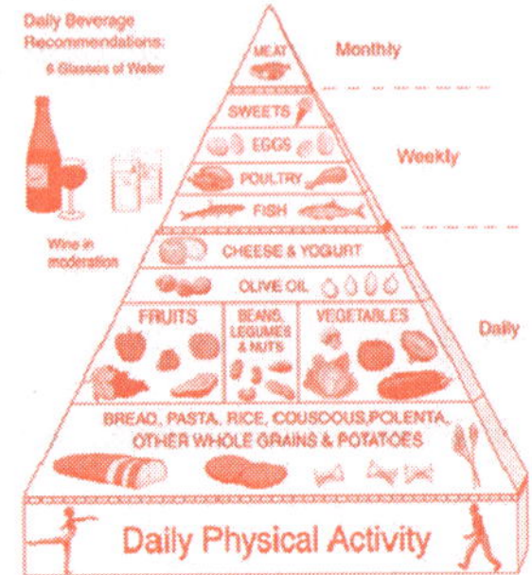

It is not possible to tell exactly what humans ate thousands of years ago, and there are no samples of 'dinosaur' meat available so that we can test the amount of saturated fat that caveman might have received from eating a chunk of roasted tyrannosaurus. However, when one reads diet recommendations today, it can be seen that in many ways old diets were more nutritious than our modern convenience-oriented diet.

● Do Chinese people like eating healthy food?

I'd say not really. Instead, they like to eat uncommon food like some strange birds or the old turtles. But as there are more and more health problems related to dieting, people tend to pay more attention to it.

● Do you care about how your food is made when you eat at a restaurant?

Better not to! I only need to enjoy what has been served, but talking about how it is cooked, it may make people scared.

● Do people in China place much importance on food safety?

For individuals, of course everyone would pay great attention to food safety. But for the manufacturers, I doubt the answer since there are some horrible scandals about food making security.

✓ Joedy 点评：

Food safety这关系到人们健康的问题，大家都会很关注吧。但是中国有句话叫"民以食为天"，很多时候美食的诱惑往往大于理性的思考，例如人们明明知道河豚有毒，果子狸带病菌，大家还是忍不住要去吃！人们明明知道炸薯条和炸鸡翅对健康没有益处，还是抵挡不住诱惑。国外的朋友都对于中国人吃rabbit, turtle, frog legs, squirrel, beaver, deer, raccoon, country pigeons感到很不可思议。

不过呢，健康始终还是很重要的，看看专家给我们什么建议。

Food safety for your family

You probably have lots of concerns about the foods you give to your child. Is it a nutritious meal? Will your child eat it? Is there too much fat? But one thing that may not cross your mind as you're slicing and dicing in the kitchen is food safety.

Why is food safety so important? Proper food preparations are necessary to prevent your family from becoming sick from food-borne illnesses caused by bacteria such as E. coli, Salmonella, Campylobacter and Listeria (which can cause symptoms such as diarrhea, fever, abdominal cramps, nausea, vomiting, and dehydration). Food safety precautions include knowing how to select foods in the grocery store, how to store them, how to cook them, and how to clean up afterward.

So what can you do to make sure your kitchen and the foods you prepare are safe? Keep reading to find out.

Buying Food

The grocery store is your first stop on the way to food safety. To ensure freshness, refrigerated items (such as meat, dairy, eggs, and fish) should be put in your cart last. Keep meats separate from other items, especially produce. If your driving home is longer than one hour, you might consider putting these items in a cooler to keep them fresh.

When purchasing packaged meat, poultry, or fish, be sure to check the expiration date on the label. Even if the expiration date is still acceptable, don't buy fish or meats that have any unusual odors or look strange.

It's also important to check inside egg cartons — make sure the eggs, which should be graded A or AA, are clean and free from cracks.

Don't buy:

fruit with broken skin (bacteria can enter through the opening in the skin and contaminate the fruit)

unpasteurized ciders or juices (they can contain harmful bacteria)

pre-stuffed fresh turkeys or chickens

再来看看普通家庭有什么好方法去ensure food safety。

How important is food safety to you?

A. Essential. I take every precaution needed and I never dry my dishes with a tea towel.

B. Very important. I never leave food out. I always make sure things are cooked. I always use separate cutting boards.

C. Important. I'm aware of the issue and do my best to prevent food poisoning. I wash my hands before touching food and use my freezer.

D. A clear list is not on my mind right now, but besides basics like washing hands, checking the expiration dates on stuff and keeping food in the freezer, my problem is that here people that work in the food business do not respect the hygiene regulations.

● How can the government supervise food safety?

Well, maybe enhancing the inspecting system can make the supervision more effective. But I don't know how it can be undertaken because it is quite a professional topic.

Cooking

● Is it important to have meals with the whole family?

Of course! It is a great chance for the whole family to share a lot of things with each other, like happiness, sorrow, and an experience at work and so on.

● Do Chinese people often eat at home?

Well, it depends. For those at work, it's hard for them to have lunch at home. They may bring their own lunch-boxes. But having dinner at home is quite a normal thing for Chinese.

● Why do people cook less now and what are the disadvantages of it?

It is because there are more and more fast-food restaurants and take-away services, which may do harm to people's health and make them lazier and lazier.

✓ Joedy 点评：

来看看一些中国朋友是如何看待dinning out的，有很多语句值得参考。

A: In my childhood dining out was a wonderful thing to me. To eat in a plush restaurant where many kinds of food can be sampled used to be a great treat to me. The <u>dreamy music, soft lighting, courteous service, and delicacies</u> served are the things to consummate the pleasure of eating. There you can order whatever you want to eat if only you have enough money on you. <u>Expensive as it may be, dining out indeed saves us a lot of trouble getting things cooked, clearing up the table and washing dirty dishes.</u> But now my interest in dining out has gradually diminished. In the first place it is not economical, and not safe. I can not but allow for the possibility of catching a disease in an eating place. The noise made by many people eating together in a restaurant can also spoil my appetite. Aside from all this, the strongest reason that keeps me from <u>having the itch to dine out</u> is my having got an excellent cook in my own house — my mother.

✓ Joedy 点评：

这一段话当中对餐厅的美好气氛以及带来的便利的描述特别的精彩，大家可以学习划线部分的句型并把他们应用到考试当中去。

B: In a bustling urban district, restaurants of every description can often be found. They satisfy us with well-prepared food and <u>save us the trouble</u> of cooking a meal at the place where we live. Most people, especially the unmarried, like to dine out, and restaurants have thus become a permanent part of the urban scene. However, in the headlong rush to turn a quick profit, restaurants, especially those second-rate ones, are likely to serve unsanitary food to their customers, a tendency much helped by the negligence in cleaning used dishes and also by the failure to keep food well-preserved. <u>It goes without saying that</u> some restaurants are virtually the breeding ground of disease-carrying germs and an infectious disease can easily  spread from a germ-carrying diseased person to a healthy one. The wide spread of infectious diseases can pose serious problems. One way around this is for the health authorities to establish rigorous regulations governing the running of a restaurant. On the other hand, restaurateurs should also have a sense of hygiene and conform to business ethics. We are all looking forward to the day when diners-out can go everywhere without fear.

✓Joedy 点评：

　　这个答案的独到之处在于深入地分析了餐厅的卫生情况可能带来的健康问题。同时，划线标注的句型特别适合考试的时候使用。

C: Some people dine out to save the trouble of preparing and cooking food by themselves, others just want to do this for a change. But I don't like dining out. Some restaurants care little about hygienic standards, taking on trouble to see whether their dinner sets are clean or dirty. Sometimes they serve tasty food but are neglectful in other respects. Diseases enter by the mouth. So it is important for us to pay attention to the sanitation of our dinner  sets and food. Insanitary dinners are sometimes harmful to our health. Though the food served at a restaurant is generally more palatable, we still have to take care to see whether the place is kept clean. Furthermore, dining out is usually a costly affair, while eating at home is, as a rule, inexpensive and safer. So I think we had better avoid dining out. If it is quite necessary to do that, it is advisable to go to a place where health <u>risks are reduced to a minimum</u>.

 D: To most people dining out seems to be a delightful experience because it can stimulate one's appetite while dining at home all the time often makes one feel bored. Sometime I also like to go out dining and try something different. When I am too tired and hungry to go on my studying in the night, I usually go to the night market for a snack. At the night market I can have a wide selection of food, such as noodles, sea foods and roast beef, which is not only spicy and savory but also good to look at. But one thing that I never neglect when dining out is the sanitation of the food offered. Everywhere in Taiwan you can see snack vendors, snack bars and various types of restaurants, but few seem to worry about whether their plates, bowls and chopsticks have been well washed or sanitized or question whether food prepared

and served under such circumstances will affect people's health. So whenever I go out to eat, the cleanliness of the place where I eat rather than the taste of the food is what really matters to me. And I hope all of us can heed the sanitation problem lest we catch diseases when we dine out.

✓Joedy 点评：

以上四个中国朋友给出的答案都不约而同地从饮食卫生方面论证了dining out的坏处，再来看看国外的朋友是如何看待这个问题的。

I Like Dining Out

I like dining out. I love to cook, but I think having a break and dining out once in a while is a great thing to do. My husband and I usually dine out once a week on his day off. I really enjoy just sitting in a restaurant and enjoying a nice meal over great conversation. And of course you have to have dessert! One of my favorite places to dine out is a place here called Southern Pit BBQ, which is fresh pulled BBQ, which they serve with cornbread, coleslaw, baked beans, and brunwick stew. Yum! I also love to go to IHOP, Applebees, Cracker Barrel, and Waffle House.

✓Joedy 点评：

大家可以看到，这个答案的可取之处在于结尾处恰如其分地给出了具体的例子，论证了dining out的乐趣。这也是考生在考试过程中可以使用的一个策略，尤其是对于第三部分的题目，适当地举出例子将会给自己的答案增色不少。

I enjoy eating out. Growing up, going out to eat was very rare for us to do. Mom did not have the money and she was a good cook anyway so she would just make all our meals. Now when I go out to eat, it feels like a special day. Kind of like I am being pampered. I get to order whatever I want and someone else cooks it! Sometimes other people's cooking tastes better when you don't have to make it! Then I get waited on with refills on drinks and asked how my dinner is. Then the best part is... I do not have to do dishes! Whew hew! That itself is worth paying the bill! Yup, I love to go out to eat. Anytime and any place!

● How do you get the information of food quality when you are shopping for food?

Well, for those fresh foods like vegetables and fruits, I just judge by their appearance; for those packed, I can only rely on the QS mark, which means Quality Safe probably.

● Do students like cooking by themselves?

Most of them may not like it I think, because their parents do not need them to do so. But I do know that some teenagers are keen on cooking but only as an interest instead of cooking every day.

● Is it necessary for students to learn to cook?

Of course it is, because sooner or later, they will live on their own. I don't think they can afford to eat out every day.

● Do children have any idea about junk food?

I think so, even though most children are attracted by fast food, especially its advertising and toys, their parents have been telling them the true value of fast food.

● Do boys have to be a good cook and what about girls?

I don't think any of them should be a good cook. They just need to know some daily cooking to support their life. But maybe boys can be better at cooking for their strong built.

● How do students learn to cook?

I think they learn to cook most likely from their parents. If some of them are really interested in cooking, they may attend some courses or go to some vocational schools.

● Do you think schools should provide cooking lessons?

That would be a good idea since most students in China have suffered a lot from their academic study. Offering cooking classes can brighten their boring study life.

● Who should be responsible for teaching children to cook, teachers or parents?

I think parents should mainly take up this responsibility since they have the closest life with their children. They can teach the children when making dinner every day, which is not a suitable time for teachers.

● Do schools have the responsibility to provide nutritious food for students?

Of course they do! They not only need to provide nutrition to the students but also have the responsibility to inspect the food they offer.

第4节　Places and Environment

Lesson 1 Part 1 听题训练

　　讲到living place，雅思口语考试比较关注考生居住的城市、居住的房屋以及房屋周围的设施例如公园等，问的问题都挺简单的。但是有些问题在考生听来，觉得很不可思议。例如，问考生为什么要在花园里种菜，考生家墙上挂着什么。这些问题一不留神就会以为自己听错了，所以现在好好读一下理解一下题目大意吧！千万不要走题。

City and town
● Are you living in a big city or a small town?
● Where do you want to live in most, the city or the small town?
● What aspects of cities do you like best?
● What are the problems most big cities are facing?
● Do you want to live in a big city or a small town when you are abroad?

House / flat (apartment)
● Do you currently live in a house or a flat / apartment?
● How long have you been living there?
● What is your house / flat / apartment like?
● What can you see through the window?
● What is on the walls of your home?
● Which part of your flat do you like / dislike most?
● How would you like to improve your apartment?
● What are your neighbors like?

Park / garden

- Do you often go to the park?

- What do people usually do in the park?

- What role do parks play in the city?

- Do many people in China have their own garden?

- What do people usually plant in the garden, flowers or vegetables?

Lesson 2 Part 1 真题点评与参考答案

City and town

- Are you living in a big city or a small town?

I live in GZ, which is one of the biggest cities in China. It has a large population and it is quite modern.

- Where do you want to live in most, the city or the small town?

I prefer to live in a big city because the life there is more interesting with all sorts of entertainment available such as pubs, shopping centers and theatres.

- **What aspects of cities do you like best?**

I think I like the humanity environment of the city best. Big cities offer us great opportunities to enjoy various forms of art and different cultures from all around the world.

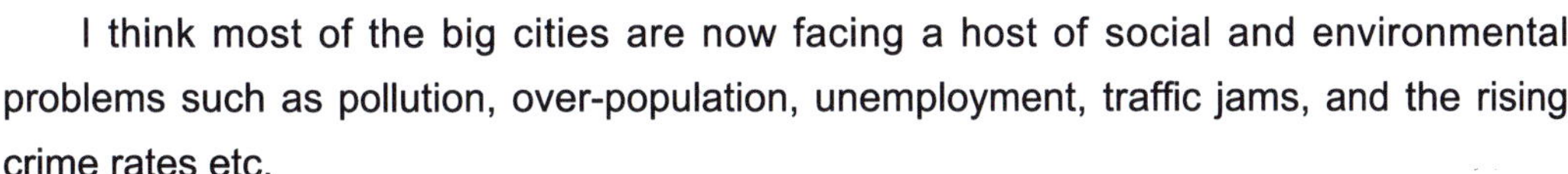

- **What are the problems most big cities are facing?**

I think most of the big cities are now facing a host of social and environmental problems such as pollution, over-population, unemployment, traffic jams, and the rising crime rates etc.

- **Do you want to live in a big city or a small town when you are abroad?**

I would definitely choose a big city so as to experience the local culture more. I believe I can better understand the country in the big cities where there are more people from different parts of the country.

House / flat (apartment)

- **Do you currently live in a house or a flat /apartment?**

I am living in an apartment near my school. It is not very big, but it is in a convenient neighborhood.

- **How long have you been living there?**

I have been living here since I came to GZ. That's to say, about ten years.

- **What is your house / flat /apartment like?**

It is still new and the facilities are running quite well. I have all the necessary furniture installed, like TV, washing machine, air-con.

- **What can you see through the window?**

I can see many trees and other buildings outside the window. I really enjoy standing by my window sometimes and just looking outside. That makes me calm.

- **What is on the walls of your home?**

I have a few pictures on the walls, because I like paintings very much. The one hanging on the wall of my bedroom is my favorite. I drew it on a journey to Tibet.

- **Which part of your flat do you like / dislike most?**

I like my room most, because it is very cozy and there is a small study which allows me to indulge in reading a lot.

● How would you like to improve your apartment?

I may renovate my room this year. I would love to repaint my walls because they are turning yellow after all these years.

● What are your neighbors like?

My neighbors are nice and friendly and we often have a small talk when we meet.

Park / garden

● Do you often go to the park?

I seldom go to the park because I am very busy working everyday and I have no time.

● What do people usually do in the park?

As far as I know, the people who often go to the park in China are senior citizens. In the park, they can take a walk, do Taiji, sing a song and so on. Actually, there are a variety ways for them to relax and keep healthy in the park.

● What role do parks play in the city?

Oh, this is a hard question. Parks, in my opinion, serves as a place for people to relax and entertain themselves. It is also a place for people to meet friends and have a get-together party.

● Do many people in China have their own garden?

Most Chinese people live in a flat. Few people in China have a garden especially those who live in the cities.

● What do people usually plant in the garden, flowers or vegetables?

If they do have a garden, I think, most people would like to plant vegetables, which can not only provide people with the non-polluted vegetables, but also lessen the economic burden of a family.

Lesson 3 Part 2 审题训练与真题讲解

★ Cue card 审题训练

Describe a historic place that interests you.

You should say:

Where it is.

How you got to know it.

When you first went there.

What is special about it.

And explain the reason why it interests you.

✓Joedy 提醒：

　　Historic place绝对是大家觉得超级难扩展的一张卡片。有些考生考前辛辛苦苦在网上或者书本里查阅了大量的资料并背下了很多描述该地方的词汇，考试时自认为讲得非常完美，但是却给了考官背答案的嫌疑，吃力却不讨好，郁闷至极！其实，大家根本不需要给太多太专业的描述，所有对于地方的描述都应该紧密地与自己的亲身感受联系起来。例如，考生要讲the Great Wall，每个人都讲Those who don't reach the Great Wall are not true men. 这些人尽皆知的大道理，有什么意思呢？考生可以放多一点笔墨在去到长城见到的景观，重点向考官分享自己的真实感受，这样更容易扩展也更容易打动考官。

　　试试吧。

★ Cue card真题点评与参考答案

China is a country with a long history and there are so many historic places. One of which I like most is the Palace Museum, which is also called Forbidden City. It's located at the center of Beijing. It was the imperial palace during the Ming and Qing Dynasties. I think every Chinese people knows Palace Museum and is proud of it, because it is part of our culture.

So when I was little, I had been dreaming of going there. I didn't make it until the year when I graduated from the university. That was 1993. I went to Beijing with three other classmates. We lived in one of the dormitory of my friend who studied in Beijing Normal University. The first place we visited is Beijing Tiananmen Square, and then the Forbidden City. I was really amazed to see how magnificent the Forbidden City is especially the splendid painted decoration on those royal architectural wonders, the grand and deluxe halls, with their surprisingly magnificent treasures. It was really impressive. I can never forget that day when I visited the Forbidden City.

Nowadays, the Forbidden City, or the Palace Museum is open to tourists from home and abroad. It is one of the places people from all over the world would like to pay a visit to if they come to China.

✓Joedy 点评：

这个historic place一旦准备好，就可以转成近年来许多热门的卡片了，例如：

> Describe your favorite tourist attraction in your country.
>
> You should say:
>
> > Where it is.
> >
> > What it is famous for.
> >
> > What people usually do there.
>
> And explain the reason why you like it.

A tourist attraction或者a place of interest 都可以讲这个historic place，考生只需要改头换面就可以了。

另外还有一张卡片叫an educational visit，其实也是可以用historic place来转换的，就说是参观这个historic place啊，非常有教育意义吧。

还有，有一张卡片是museum，是不是也可以用historic place转换？

好吧，现在再提供一些资料给大家，希望对大家开扩思路有帮助。

The Ancient Town of Zhouzhuang（周庄）

Zhouzhuang, honored as "the No. 1 Water Town in China", is an ancient town in the south of the Yangtze River of China. This peaceful and secluded town, located in the southeast of Suzhou City, are scattered with buildings of ancient style. After over 900 years of ups and downs, the architectural styles of the water town are well preserved and pretty much the same as what they were in the past.

The crisscrossing rivers, along which stand buildings constructed hundreds of years ago, are the most striking feature in the town of Zhouzhuang. In fact, over 60% of the buildings across the town were built in the Ming and Qing Dynasties. In this tiny ancient town of merely 0.47 sq-kilometers, there are approximately one hundred classical houses and over 60 brick carving gate towers. The most representative building is Shen's House, which is a courtyard house with the Qing Dynasty styles. The overall structure of the house is in neat formation, and different architectural styles can be found in various parts.

There are a total of 14 ancient bridges built in the Yuan, Ming and Qing dynasties over the rivers in the town. The most famous scenic spots include: Fu'an Bridge, which is the only existing three-dimensional structure integrating a bridge and a tower in the south of the Yangtze River; the Twin Bridge, which is a uniquely structured "two-in-one" bridge; and religious sites like Chengxu Taoist Temple and Quanfu Teaching Temple etc. — Culture Heritage Conservation, American Government Award and the title of "the world's most charming water town" etc.

Badaling — The Great Wall of China （八达岭长城）

The Great Wall is probably the most often visited destination in China for foreign tourists, and Badaling is the site of the most visited section of the Great Wall of China, approximately 50 miles (80 km) northwest of Beijing city in Yanqing County, which is within the Beijing municipality. The portion of the wall running through the site was built during the Ming Dynasty, along with a military outpost reflecting the location's strategic importance.

The portion of the wall at Badaling has undergone heavy restoration, and in 1957 it was the first section of the wall to open to tourists. Now visited annually by millions, the immediate area has seen significant development, including hotels, restaurants, and a cable car. The recently completed Badaling Expressway connects Badaling with Beijing city.

It was here that President Richard Nixon and his wife, accompanied by Vice Premier Li Xiannian, visited on February 24, 1972, during his historic journey to China. It was also the part of the wall climbed by Mao Zedong and other 370 international dignitaries and celebrities.

Badaling and the expressway were the sites of the finishing circuit of the Urban Road Cycling Course in the 2008 Summer Olympics. Laps of the circuit passed through gates in the wall.

Most visitors encounter the Great Wall at Badaling, its most-photographed manifestation, 70km northwest of Beijing. The scenery is raw and yields choice views of the wall snaking archetypally into the distance over undulating hills.

The city of Xi'an （西安）

The city of Xi'an, in central China, is historically very important.

Around 650 to 700 AD, it was the capital of the Chinese Empire, the seat of the Tang Dynasty, and the eastern terminus of the great "Silk Road" trading route between China and the Mediterranean. It was then the largest city in the world, with over two million inhabitants, a quarter of whom were foreigners, and archaeologists have estimated that it contained about 60,000 separate trading establishments.

In 1974, it became famous again as the city where an army of life-sized terracotta warriors was discovered, buried to guard an ancient emperor's grave.

✓Joedy 点评：

考生看完这三个地方的介绍可能会感叹：怎么可能在短短的一分钟的准备时间当中想出那么多的细节呢！其实只有在考前多去收集机经并且通过电视或者报刊杂志等途径积累相关的信息，在真正考试的时候才能够如鱼得水，发挥出色。我相信，chance favors the prepared mind.

描述地点的话题一般要求考生描述自己去过或者想去的一个地方，大家可以用以下常见的思路。

1. Where is it located?

2. What is your first impression of it?

3. What is it like?

4. What can people do there?

描述地方的时候，最忌讳的就是死板地介绍这个地方的外貌、功能、设备等等，要让听者眼前一亮，最好是分享自己去到此地方的经历以及亲身感受。例如，是被当地的小吃snacks吸引了呢？还是沉浸在tranquil and serene scenery宁静的风光里呢？或者是被丰富的recreational activities 休闲活动吸引了？又可能是在这个地方发生的一件事令自己对此地方印象深刻？地点不应该是静止的，每个要介绍的地点，都要说出感情来，也就是分享自己与这个地点的故事。所以，大家平时多点尝试描述某个地方发生的事，会得到意想不到的收获。

Lesson 4 Part 3 听题训练

✓Joedy 提醒：

　　Culture and tradition是雅思口语考试Part 3关注重点之一，问的问题无非都是"保护传统历史的重要性"，"我们国家保护传统的现状"，"保护传统的方法"等等。当然，Part 3的问题考官问得非常灵活，考官会根据考生的表现随时调整问题的难度，也就是说，同样的意思，考官可能会用不同的句式或者用词。一旦考官改变了措辞，考生可能会无法立刻抓住考官的意思。

　　所以，大家要多读读下面给大家提供的关于history的问题，并试着把这些问题用不同的方式复述出来。

Historic site
● Do you like traveling? Why do people like traveling?
● Which places are Chinese people most interested in visiting? Why?
● Are there many historic places in China?
● What suggestions do you give to foreigners who visit these historic places?
● Do people especially the young like traveling to the historic sites?
● Should people pay to visit the historic places?
● Is it necessary to learn history?
● Through what ways can people get to know history?
● Do you like movies about history?
● What kind of museums do Chinese like?
● Should public museums charge fees?
● Who is responsible for building public facilities?

✓Joedy 提醒：

雅思口语考试关注的社会话题除了"传统和文化"，还有"环保"。讲到places，肯定会提到tourism和traveling这两个方面，而tourism的发展对local place势必带来影响。以下的问题有一些关键词，例如：相对于artificial scenery（人文景观）而言的natural scenery（自然景观）；positive and negative impact（正面和负面影响）；advantages and disadvantages（优缺点）。这些词大家一定要会读，而且要读正确，不然考官读出来我们是反应不过来的。

Tourism
● Where do people like going for traveling?
● Do people like visiting natural scenery?
● How is the tourism in your country?
● Why is it necessary to develop tourism?
● What is the positive and negative impact of the tourism on the city?
● What are the disadvantages of living around the tourist attraction?
● What has the Chinese government done to solve the problems brought by tourism?

✓Joedy 提醒：

　　刚才已经提过了，"环保"是雅思口语考试很关注的题材，近几年global warming以及greenhouse effects大家都经常听到吧！2008年那场重大冰灾雪灾，让extreme weather这个话题又热了起来，所以大家准备好来谈谈对于气候变化的看法吧。

Climate
● What are the differences between the four seasons in your country?
● Would you choose to live in a country with distinct seasons?
● What season do people in your hometown like best?
● Do you prefer cold weather or warm weather?
● What is the relationship between weather and people's work?
● What is the difference between working in winter and summer?
● What kinds of jobs are restricted by weather?
● How has the weather changed in China these years?
● What do you think of the greenhouse effect?
● What is the cause for global warming?
● What should we do to solve this problem?

Lesson 5 Part 3 真题讲解与参考答案

Historic site

● Do you like traveling? Why do people like traveling?

Yes, I like travelling a lot. I think people can learn a lot from travelling. For instance, travelling can broaden one's horizon; provide people more opportunities to experience different cultures and customs and so on.

● Which places are Chinese people most interested in visiting? Why?

As for the place people like to go, I think "different people, different minds". But for me, I prefer to go to some places that are quite different from the ones I know. Say, some natural places like Jiuzhaigou.

✓Joedy 点评：

如果发现考官问的问题非常广泛，广泛到考生根本没办法给出确切答案的话，先不要急着放弃，考生可以先直接回应考官，然后根据自己所知道的给出自己的答案就OK了。

✓Joedy 挑选了另外两个考生的回答：

Lhasa（拉萨）

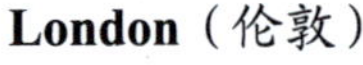

Lhasa is the city I want to visit most.

The mild and pleasant climate in central Tibet makes this area available for tourists year around. This route offers the epitome of Tibet with some of the most impressive visions: snow-capped mountains and holy lakes, splendid monasteries and palaces, original villages and unsophisticated people. With the better road conditions and accommodations along the way, it is now the most popular route.

London（伦敦）

London was definitely my favorite city. I love the fact that the museums are free, the drum and bass music is fantastic, there's heaps to do, and the fact that the people speak English is a plus after having difficulty being understood for months. I've managed to remember to look the correct way before crossing so I don't end up being smashed by a car because I looked the wrong way. It is a very vibrant and European city, and I truly love London. If I were to move to another city, it would surely be London.

- **Are there many historic places in China?**

Yeah. There are a great many historic places in China because as it is known, China is a country with a long history. Many of the historic places are famous around the world, such as the Great Wall, the Tiananmen Square.

- **What suggestions do you give to foreigners who visit these historic places?**

The advice I'd like to give people from other countries is to do some research before they come to the historic place they want. Get as much information as possible in terms of weather, what to see, how to get there, what to learn etc.

- **Do people, especially the young like traveling to the historic sites?**

It's really hard to say who likes to go to historic places. As for me, I would prefer to visit natural places rather than historic places. Even though people can learn a lot from the historic places, but I reckon, it is a bit boring and people may feel a bit depressed sometimes.

- **Should people pay to visit the historic places?**

I think people should pay for their visit to the historic places because the historic places need maintaining and repairing, which certainly cost a lot of human resources. Besides, the fees tourists provided will reduce the burden of the government so that they can invest more money on other public facilities.

✓ **Joedy 点评:**

这个问题的答案可以直接使用于所有同类问题中，凡是问到 public facilities，例如library, museum, park等是否应该免费向公众开放时，都可以如范文这样回答，这叫举一反三。

- **Is it necessary to learn history?**

Yes, definitely it is necessary for people to learn history. Only when people know the history well can they make good use of what they have learned from history to do what they can do in today's society.

✓ **Joedy 点评:**

很多考生不知道如何回答这个问题，因为他们本身就搞不懂为什么要学习历史保护传统文化。现在就来看看，到底学习历史有什么重要性。

Studying History? Yes, it is necessary

History, as a sum of all the events, is very important because it guides our actions in the present. This is true not only for the individual (imagine what would have happened to you, had your parents never met, or had your parents raised you with different values), but also for large societies as well (how would the U.S. be different, for example, if it had lost the American Revolution, or if the Spanish had founded the colonies of North America that became the United States?). In both cases the United States as we know would not exist.

Learning history is of great importance for the reason that it helps us make sense of the world around us. It is the only way we can understand who we are and how we got to be that way. Similarly, the only way we can understand others is by studying their past. If we don't understand what made them who they are — in terms of how they think and act — we will make all sorts of mistakes in our interactions with them. Think of how you treat people differently based on how you know them. The same is true for countries when it comes to diplomacy. To establish a long-lasting partnership with another country, we need to take time to truly study and understand their past.

✓Joedy 点评:

这一高分答案的突出特点是逻辑性非常强：首先直接给出观点：历史帮助人们理解周围的世界；然后围绕观点解释：1.历史帮助理解自己；2.历史帮助理解周围的人。而加分点在于把观点升华到国家外交的高度。总地来说，这个答案还是遵循了之前所说的point+why／how+example的基本原则。

● **Through what ways can people get to know history?**

There are actually many ways people can learn history. For instance, people can learn it from school, reading books, visiting museums, watching movies or surfing the internet etc.

● **Do you like movies about history?**

Not really. Most movies about history are rigid and boring. I could never have any fun while watching one. I remember once my friends dragged me to the cinema and watched one famous movie about the history back in Qing Dynasty. I almost fell asleep. So I am really not so into those movies.

● **What kind of museums do Chinese like?**

I don't know what other people would like. But personally, if asked to choose, I prefer history museum, because from history museum, people can learn the ancient ways of life, works of art, architecture and so on.

Should public museums charge fees?

It may be better if public museums open for everyone. In this way, the number of visitors to museum will greatly increase, therefore, people can learn more about science, history and arts. It will be beneficial for the children's development as well.

Who is responsible for building public facilities?

Of course the government should take the responsibility to establish more public facilities because the job of government is to serve the people and make people's life better and better.

Tourism

Where do people like going for traveling?

Different people may have different choices. Some people especially people living in the city like visiting some natural places like Hainan Island and Jiuzhai Valley. While others are into some historic places such as Beijing and Xi'an.

Do people like visiting natural scenery?

I think so. Some famous tourist attractions famous for natural beauty are crowed with visitors during holidays. It was reported that a total of about 100,000 tourists entered one natural park in Hunan Province in just one day. I guess people really like natural places for the breathtaking scenery which people can never see in the city.

How is the tourism in your country?

As far as I know, the tourism in China is developing rapidly. It has become more and more prosperous. Every year, millions of tourists come to China for experiencing the profound history and culture, which brings about great profits. Also, many Chinese begin to travel outside China, which can greatly help boost tourism as well.

Why is it necessary to develop tourism?

There are several reasons for it and I think the most important reason is that it helps promote the understanding and communication between different cultures. With more and more foreign visitors coming to China and more and more Chinese traveling abroad, people can understand China more and we Chinese can learn a lot from other countries.

What is the positive and negative impact of the tourism on the city?

Just like the old saying goes, "Every coin has two sides." Developing tourism is no exception. It has both negative and positive influence on the city. The good points are as the answer to question four above. The bad points are as follows: for one thing, it may destroy some natural resource. For another, it causes more serious problems like air pollution and traffic problems and so on.

- **What are the disadvantages of living around the tourist attraction?**

The weakness of living around the tourist attraction is it is too noisy, besides, there are more traffic jams than any other places. Another bad point is people may not enjoy fresh air and clean water.

- **What has the Chinese government done to solve the problems brought by tourism?**

The Chinese government has made great effort to solve these problems. For example, they have limited the amount of visitors per day in some natural attractions, such as, Jiuzhai Valey. Moreover, they encourage a green tourism and call on people to protect the environment while travelling.

Climate

- **What are the differences between the four seasons in your country?**

In my hometown, there are four distinct seasons. Spring, summer, autumn and winter. Spring is the time when everything blooms; summer is the time for people to go swimming; autumn is the harvest season when farmers are busy obtaining what they have paid in Spring. Winter is the white world. It is also the high time people enjoy skiing.

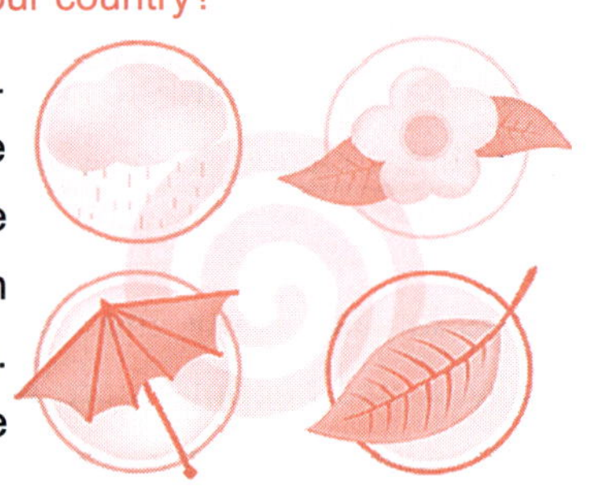

- **Would you choose to live in a country with distinct seasons?**

Yes, absolutely. I can enjoy the blossom of flowers in spring, the fun water sports in summer, the cool air in autumn and the exciting skiing in winter. It is so wonderful to have different activities and different feelings in different seasons.

- **What season do people in your hometown like best?**

I guess spring is the one people like best, because, you know, in winter, everyone has to wear thick clothes, pants, hats and mitten. And everywhere we look around is white. However, when spring comes, everything begins to turn green, which brings

hope to people. Most importantly, people begin to take off heavy clothes, which will make us feel light both mentally and physically.

● Do you prefer cold weather or warm weather?

I like warm weather better because I don't need to wear too many heavy or thick clothes. In the warm spring, I can act fast and think fast.

● What is the relationship between weather and people's work?

The weather has a great impact on humans and their work as well. As a Chinese proverb says, "Spring makes one sleepy; autumn exhausted; summer drowsy." That means different seasons give people different feelings which influences people's working efficiency.

● What is the difference between working in winter and summer?

That's a really hard question. I think there are many differences between working in winter and summer. Say, the uniform people wear must be different. People need to protect themselves from getting frozen, so they would wear thick uniforms.

● What kinds of jobs are restricted by weather?

As far as I can see, construction work is greatly restricted by weather. In the scorching summer, construction workers need a break after every 2 hours' continuous work in the sun, or else they might get sun burnt or heatstroke.

● How has the weather changed in China these years?

According to some experts, in the last few years, weather patterns over China have undergone significant changes, shifting from clear, warmer and drier weather at the beginning of the winter to the current conditions featuring widespread low-temperature, frozen rain, snow and ice.

● What do you think of the greenhouse effect?

It has a negative impact on earth and human life because it raises the temperature of the earth, which will lead to a lot of natural disasters like the heat wave that killed a hundred people in India this summer. We have been undergoing a longer and longer summer in these years and I am afraid that things will get more and more serious.

● What is the cause for global warming?

Many factors contribute to global warming. For one thing, carbon dioxide accounts for most of the greenhouse gases in the atmosphere. Another important factor is human activity such as releasing car exhaust, which has increased the amount of greenhouse gases in the atmosphere. These gases in turn send more heat back to the earth, causing a further increase in temperatures.

● What should we do to solve this problem?

There are certainly a lot of good ways to solve this problem and reducing the number of private cars is one effective way. Our government has taken effective measures such as raising the purchase tax to strangle people's strong desire of buying a new private car. People are encouraged to use the renewable energy and we are becoming more aware of the importance of protecting the environment.

第5节　Transport and Traffic

Lesson 1 Part 1 听题训练

Traffic属于"衣食住行"里最后一环，但是却一点都不能忽视。城市里的交通方式有很多种，常见的有：bus, subway, taxi, private car等。如之前所说的，雅思口语考试很关注"环保"概念，所以近几年除了考walking之外，就重点考了bicycle这种非常环保的出行方式。当然，最近driving private car这个话题有慢慢变得重要的趋势，但是bicycle始终还是不能忽略的。好好听题吧。加油！

Traffic

- How did you come here today?

- How many kinds of transports are there in your hometown?

- What is your favorite way of transport in your living city?

- Is cycling popular in your country? Why?

- Do all children in your country learn bicycle?

- What are the advantages of riding bicycles compared to driving cars?

- Is it safe to ride bicycles in your living city?

- How is the transport fare in your hometown?

Lesson2 Part 1 真题点评与参考答案

Traffic

- **How did you come here today?**

I came here by taxi because I had to make sure that I wouldn't be late.

- **How many kinds of transports are there in your hometown?**

Well, in my hometown Guangzhou, there are mainly three types of transportation, bus, metro and taxi.

- **What is your favorite way of transport in your living city?**

I like traveling by metro mostly because it is faster, there are seldom any jams, and it's more comfortable and always on time.

● Is cycling popular in your country? Why?

It is quite popular in some small cities since there is no perfect system of transportation; but in big cities, cycling is not as popular as in the countryside for the heavy traffic.

● Do all children in your country learn bicycle?

I can say that at least there is nobody I know who can't ride a bicycle.

● What are the advantages of riding bicycles compared to driving cars?

It is more convenient, you don't need to worry about the parking lot. And it is more environment-friendly since it produces no waste gas.

● Is it safe to ride bicycles in your living city?

I don't think so. There are too many cars running fast or even crazily on every road. Everyone needs to be particularly careful when they are cycling.

● How is the transport fare in your hometown?

Well, I think it's quite reasonable compared with housing. And the government has put some very favorable policies on transporting.

Lesson 3 Part 2 审题训练与真题讲解

★ Cue card审题训练

Describe an experience of being caught in a traffic jam.

You should say:

    When it happened.

    Where it happened.

    How you passed the time while waiting.

And explain how you felt about that traffic jam.

✓Joedy 提醒：

    考生在看卡片的时候一定要注意卡片上标注的时态，那是一个陷阱，一不留神就会审题出错。像这一张卡片，是让考生描述an experience of being stuck in a traffic jam，下面的小标题都是用了过去时，证明是要求考生讲过去经历的某一次塞车，而不是笼统地讲城市里的塞车情况。以前有一张卡片是这样的，

> Describe a happy family event.
>
> You should say:
>
> When it was.
>
> What you did.
>
> Whom you spent it with.
>
> And explain why it was a happy experience.

很多同学都讲了"年夜饭"，而且都用了一般现在时来讲述，大家注意，这个卡片是用过去时描述的，也就是让考生描述某一次特定的 family event，即使要讲"年夜饭"，也应该特定讲某一年的年夜饭，不能笼统地讲。

好了，现在来想想有没有某一次的塞车让你印象深刻？

★ Cue card真题点评与参考答案

It was a terrible traffic jam on one of the main roads of Guangzhou, Guangzhou Avenue. It was about two weeks ago. At that time I was in a taxi ready to see off one of my friends at the airport. The traffic was ok at the beginning, but two minutes later, the taxi slowed down and what I didn't want to see happened — traffic jam. I at once sent a SMS to my friend, telling her that I might arrive a little later and promised I would try my best to meet her at the airport. Then, I started my boring and seem-endless waiting. It totally took me half an hour to get rid of the big jam and the taxi fee was crazily high — 190 RMB. But luckily I got to the airport on time and could send my love to my dearest friend. Personally, I do hate traffic jams. But sometimes it is people who are in great hurry that cause traffic jams, just like me.

Lesson 4 Part 3 听题训练

✓Joedy 提醒：

交通问题是Part 3"环保"主题里的一个分支，traffic问题几乎涵盖了Part 3所有的问题类型，例如：对比类（compare the difference between being stuck on a bus or in a private car）；描述类（the traffic situation in your hometown）；解决类（what should be done about the traffic situation）；态度类（do you think it a good idea to have private cars）；展望类（What is the transport going to be like in the future）。

大家要仔细听清楚题目类别，只有听清了才能有重点地去论证自己的观点！

Traffic
●Can you compare the differences between being stuck on a bus or in a private car?
●How is the traffic situation in your hometown?
●When do traffic jam usually happen?
●Has the transport changed much in these years?
●What influence may traffic bring to our environment?
●What do you think should be done about the traffic situation in the city?
●Do you think it a good idea for people to have private cars?
●What benefits do public transports bring to the traffic in a city?
●Should the government be responsible for the traffic system?
●Does it help to ease the traffic situation if more expressways and flyovers are built in the city?
●Do you think vehicles of different sizes should pay different tax?
●What is the transport going to be like in the future?

Traffic

● Can you compare the differences between being stuck on a bus or in a private car?

Well, I can do a lot of things like reading and listening while being stuck on a bus but while being stuck in a private car, I may have to concentrate on the driving, with some music probably.

● How is the traffic situation in your hometown?

Well, it's horrible. Since the Asian Games are coming in 2010, the government is undertaking some improvement projects on some of the main roads in Guangzhou. It could be totally stuck even at 4p.m..

● When do traffic jam usually happen?

During rush hours of course. Especially around those CBD areas, the traffic may begin at around 4:30 in the afternoon.

✓Joedy 点评:

来看看一个生活在广州的外国友人是如何描述他对广州交通状况的看法的。

What's wrong with the traffic in China?

The traffic situation in China is something of incredibility and mystery. Everyday when I come across traffic jam on the bus, I am amazed as to how cars and buses manage to squeeze themselves onto the road, not to mention moving or even functioning. However, I was shocked to hear, one of my students told me a striking statistics, 300 people are killed on the roads in China everyday. This is the biggest road accident death toll in the world. This is absolutely not something China can be proud of. Instead, it is something needs immediate improvement. From my observation there appears to be a number of issues that are related to the statistics.

Firstly, surprisingly, although they do exist in Guangzhou, citizens are not in the slightest bit interested in abiding by them. In other words, the traffic regulations are not being executed and people do not realize what they are doing is actually wrong. It is not unusual to see a motorbike riding on the pedestrian footpath, or a car going up the wrong way of the street, or even cars blatantly driving through red lights at an intersection. It seems to be a matter of education and people need to be educated as to the laws of the road, and a strict enforcement of them should be ensured.

Secondly, to some drivers in China, the concept of "Giving Way" seems unheard of. The only time to give way is when he or she knows that they are about to hit the other car and then it is more like an emergency stop instead of a polite and self-conscious one! This method was probably infallible in the past when only a few cars existed, but now it becomes the main cause of the major traffic problems. The situation here in China is that all traffic will just enter onto the road，taking no consideration of other traffic behind on the main road. This again results into a huge 'bottleneck' and everyone comes to grinding halt or standstill, or even worse someone touches another car!

Thirdly, the problem with buses can also be serious in China. Their method of driving is something out of the Dark Ages. I was shocked to see how they place the vehicle into neutral at a certain speed and then just sit on the brake. This is not only totally dangerous, as the passengers have to hold onto something for dear life as the bus lurches forward every time the driver presses

the brake, but also it would be costing the bus companies thousands of RMB in brake maintenance every year!

Fourthly, the actions from the government to address the traffic problem leave so much to be desired. It is my understanding that most of the large cities in China have a traffic problem. Looking at how Guangzhou has tried to solve this problem is by building more roads and introducing road regulations. The only problem with this is that the more roads you build, the more cars people use, and when you place restrictions on the use of certain roads then you are forcing all the traffic in one direction and to use the same roads, thus creating a bigger problem. When you build more major roads, the secondary or subsidiary roads are forgotten and not used.

People who have come to visit Guangzhou may feel as amazed as I did at the number of roads built on top of each other, and how unattractive it looks for the city. In order to ease the heavy traffic burden on the road, the use of smaller roads should be encouraged — linking roads. So not everyone is forced to use the same main road at once and thus causing a logistical nightmare. A car is a status symbol in China, the more wealth that people make, the more they will want to show their success by buying a car. Therefore the problem is going to get much worse. The traffic and transport problems need to be addressed soon rather than later. Let's hope some forward thinking well be done and the cities of China will be great places to live in.

✓Joedy 点评：

上文分别从交通法规的执行，市民的交通礼让意识，公交车问题以及政府的不明智解决对策等4个方面描述了中国交通的四种情况。每一个观点都可以作为考生回答雅思口语考试问题的参考。每段的黑体部分是topic sentence，也就可以作为考生回答问题时候的point。可想而知，外国人的"总分"即从笼统到具体的观念是多么根深蒂固。如果要在考试的时候跟考官make sense，这样的回答结构是不可不学的。

● Has transport changed much in these years?

Well, the opening of the new metro routes seems have to helped ease the transport, however, the increasing number of private cars has made no change in the traffic.

● What influence might traffic bring to our environment?

Most importantly, the emitted gas from the cars worsens the environment; meanwhile, there may be some noise pollution in the area where horn blowing is allowed.

● What do you think should be done about the traffic situation in the city?

For one thing, there should be some transport extension projects to ease the burden being put on the current roads. For another thing, I do think that driving restriction according to car numbers would also do good to the traffic situation.

✓**Joedy** 点评：

再来看看专家在解决上海交通问题时所提出的方案，对大家拓展思路有很大帮助。好好看看！

Solving the Traffic Problems in Shanghai

The recent development strategy as to solving the traffic problems in Shanghai is as follows:

1. Improve capacity of traffic system of the road and transport.

Shanghai's developing into an international economic city must be facilitated by the improved road capacity. Thus, a comprehensive traffic planning of Shanghai is put forward: set up the highly-efficient, unobstructed urban road system made up by the fast arterial highways, main arterial highways, the secondary arterial highways and branch roads in conformity with the city layout and function, meeting the constantly increasing city traffic demand. The plan aims for an orderly and rational urban system which is continuously developing.

2. Have priority to develop public transport.

The city traffic structure is a question with key nature. Along with the traffic network and management level, what determines the core of the efficiency level of the traffic is the distribution between various kinds of traffic ways of the total resource of the road, namely traffic structure. Walking, bicycle, public transport and cars are four main means of traffic. For the same volume of passenger transport, public transportation needs much less road areas than other means of transportation. This fully indicates that the public transport is a kind of most economic traffic way for the resource of the road. Nearly every large city of the world considers having priority for public transportation and compressing the traffic demand of the small cars as the main strategy for the city traffic. Shanghai is densely populated, the per capita traffic area is rather low and the public transit wagon flow density has already been very high, but passenger traffic demand is still very high. So the comprehensive traffic planning of Shanghai is put forward: With "public transport having priority" as the urban passenger traffic basic policy of traffic: Accelerate the construction of the urban track traffic system for even larger capacity, form and regard rail transportation as backbones, have the passenger traffic network based on the public transport of ground. In the center of the city, control private car and motorcycle and make the bicycle become the intra-regional main means of transportation.

To improve the public transit system of ground, the measure

proposed that should be taken immediately is:

1) Invest 1.5-2.0 hundred million, renew more than 2000 public transit overage buses within one to two years. Upgrade all the now existing small horsepower of buses in about five years.

2) Guarantee to increase about 300 new cars every year within ten years to come, and assort the parking and maintain facilities correspondingly.

3) Establish the view that public transit has priority. From the angle of convenience to change buses, improve position of the bus stations of the public transit; The newly- built road must be first considered to serve for the public transit; fast public transport is first considered to go on the newly-built fast arterial highways.

4) Set up the operating mechanism for the self-development of the public transit. Adjust the fee regularly according to the cost, but the government can't cancel the financial subsidy, and should legislate to guarantee the policy; public transit itself should set up competitive system, and improve the service and management.

3. Control vehicle development and vehicle usage appropriately.

The vehicle owning amount of Shanghai has still presented faster growth under the controlling doubly of the administration and economic means in recent years and as a result the city traffic is becoming more and more crowded. On one hand we must accelerate the construction of the infrastructure in the future; on the other hand we should pay attention to the development strategy of traffic at the same time.

For meeting the requirements of different purpose of going, different distance of going and different economy level, vehicle owning amount will develop further. The usage of taxis, private cars, unit scheduled buses and cars are about to increase further. So we should control the going out of officer's car of unit from the policy. For this reason, the development of the total amount of vehicles should be a development under appropriate control. The speed of the development of automobile should be in conformity with the construction speed of urban roads, and also in conformity with each regional traffic condition in the city. The policy that "to have priority to develop public transport, and control the car traffic appropriately" should be carried out.

As for the control of the car growth in the center district, there is very good successful experience in Hong Kong and Singapore. On the whole there are two ways of control. They are controlling the purchases and the usage of the mobile vehicle. The former policy includes for example imposing vehicle purchase commodity and limiting quota by means of administration, etc. Flexibly policies can be adapted to the area with heavy traffic to control the usage of vehicle.

There are some measures that in this respect can be adopted:

1) Regional restriction.

2) Charge in the area, namely the cars must hold the special pass to enter the controlled area. In order to obtain this pass, the owner of the car must pay the fees at 10% of the price of vehicle every year.

3) Different region has different charge for car parking.

4) Different charging for the region where crosses the river.

5) For the bicycle, implement the policy that besides special-purpose roads for bicycles, forbid the bicycle to enter central business area, and should also charge different parking fee for bicycles in different districts.

● Do you think its a good idea for people to have private cars?

It is a good idea for long distance traveling since you don't have to worry about being late for buses or trains. But for daily routines, the public transport, especially the metro, is a very good alternative.

● What benefits do public transports bring to the traffic in a city?

It can help consume a large number of passengers on the roads; it can also offer people some very cheap options for traveling.

● Should the government be responsible for the traffic system?

Yes, they should probably take up the majority of the responsibility, but individuals ought not to ignore their necessity of being polite drivers.

- Does it help to ease the traffic situation if more expressways and flyovers are built in the city?

Of course! But maybe it will lead to more private car owners, which has actually happened before. The more convenient the driving is, the more car owners there may be.

- Do you think vehicles of different sizes should pay different tax?

Well, it's really hard to say. I'm not a person who is good at taxation, but maybe it will make those jumbo-size car owners think they have sort of privilege.

- What is the transport going to be like in the future?

I can only say it may develop in two directions, worse or better, depending on what the government and individuals will do.

第6节　Habits and Hobbies

Lesson 1 Part 1 听题训练

雅思口语考试中对于"爱好"类的题材几乎全部都考过了。我们根本没办法预料考官会偏向哪一种爱好，尽管有些时候个别考生成功通过暗示把考官引导到自己擅长的话题去，但是大多数时候考生还是会遇到一个自己完全不感兴趣或者从来没接触过的话题。所以，没有办法中的办法，我们只能把网撒大一点点，把常见的话题都准备一下，起码有所了解，有备无患。

接下来我概括了大量关于hobbies的各类话题，大家开声读一下，复述一下，然后顺便思考一下如何作答吧。

Music
• Do you like music? What kind of music do you like?
• When do you listen to the music?
• Did you often listen to the music when you were a child?
• Do you play any musical instrument?
• Do you think it's necessary to offer a music course in high school?
• What is the influence of high tech on music?
• Do you think songs composed through computer will replace those by musicians?

Computer and internet

- Do you often use computer? What do you usually use computer for?

- What are the advantages and disadvantages of using computer?

- What are the good ways of learning computer?

- How do the elderly learn computer?

- When did you surf on the internet for the first time?

- Is the information on the Internet reliable?

- How can people avoid false information?

- Do you like writing letters? Who do you write to the most?

- What type of letters is the most difficult one to write?

- Which do you prefer, sending e-mails or writing letters?

- Do you like to receive letters or phone calls?

Shopping

- Do you like shopping?
- When do you go shopping?
- Which kind of things do you like to buy?
- What kinds of shops do you like going to?
- Which is your favorite way of shopping?
- Can you recommend a good shop for foreign visitors to Guangzhou?
- Are the shops the same to the shops decades ago?
- Is shopping very important to people? Why?

Sports

- How do you keep fit and healthy? What sports do you usually do?
- What is the most popular sport in your country?
- Which kind of sports do people in your hometown like?
- Which is the most important sport in China?
- Do you think children should learn sports at school?
- What is the difference between the sports boys do and those girls do?
- Do you like swimming? Where can you swim near your home?
- Is swimming a popular sport in your country?
- What benefits can swimming bring to people?

<table>
<tr><td align="center">Weekend</td></tr>
</table>

- What do you usually do at weekends?
- Where do you usually go at weekends?
- Some people do part-time job at weekends. Do you agree?
- Do you think it acceptable that the employers have the employees work at weekends?
- Do you think the employees will accept working at weekends?

<table>
<tr><td align="center">Holidays and traveling</td></tr>
</table>

- When was your last holiday?
- What do you like or hate to do in holidays?
- What do people do in Chinese festivals?
- Do people send presents in holidays? Is holiday important?
- Do you think there should be more holidays in the future?
- Do you like traveling?
- Do you like going traveling alone or with friends?
- What problems will people encounter during the journey?
- What should be taken into consideration when traveling abroad?
- Do you think tourism has bad effect on the local people?

Art and museum / art gallery

- Which is your favorite form of art, such as painting and sculpture?

- What is the significance and value of art?

- Did you learn any form of art when you were a child?

- How do Chinese appreciate art from other countries?

- Would you like to visit a museum to enjoy art?

- Did you ever go to the museum or art gallery when you were a child?

- Tell me an experience that you went to the museum or art gallery.

- What do you think you can learn from visiting museum and gallery?

- What role does museum play in a city?

- What should be done to attract more visitors to the museum and gallery?

Reading

- Do you like reading? What books do you usually read? Why?
- Do you like reading academic books?
- Why do some people not like reading?
- Did you read any books when you were a child?
- Do you think children in China nowadays like reading?
- What books do children like reading now?
- What influence does reading have on children?

Daily routines

- What is your daily routine?
- What time do you usually get up?
- What do you usually do in the evening?
- Do you follow the same routine every night?
- Was your nightlife the same as that of now?
- Where do you like to go in the evening?
- Is there any difference between your routine now and in your childhood?
- What time in a day do you like best?
- How would you like to change your life?
- Will you change your routines as the four seasons changing?

Lesson 2 Part 1 真题点评与参考答案

Music

● Do you like music? What kind of music do you like?

Yes, I do. I think music can help me relax very well. Usually I like listening to pop music, sometimes country and western, they are both easy to understand. Blues and jazz are good too, they make me feel classy when I listen to them.

✓Joedy 点评：

看看下面不同人对于他们喜好的音乐的描述，很简单的表达，大家学一下。

I enjoy listening to **Rock** and **pop music**. These types of music can give me a calm feeling, or they might have a dance-like quality. When driving a car, I always listen to these types of music that are usually played on the local radio stations.

I am quite into a type of music called **alternative**, which may sound unfamiliar to most people. It can be very different. Some of it is calm and some of it is hard sounding. It may also have a little of both. It is the variations of it that attract me most.

Techno is the form of music I have been listening to recently. It usually has computer-generated sounds and beats with very fast tempo. It is a retro 80s fashion to listen to techno.

Young people like me have special feelings for **R&B** and **Dance**. They usually have a techno like beat and usually have a lot of vocals. We often dance with the music in clubs.

I think I am one of the small group of people who are keen on **Hard and Metal**, which usually consists of a lot of bass and other background noise. The songs usually don't have a happy feeling to them although, they have been around for a while.

I am fond of some soft types of music like **New Age**, **Light**, and **Jazz**.

They are often sad, but comforting. Whenever I feel upset and depressed, they smooth my mind.

I like **rap music**, and I rap a lot myself. Contrary to popular thinking that rap is skin-deep and nothing but noise, I take rap as a way for young people to express their anger and dissatisfaction with the society, which is something worth noting.

- **When do you listen to music?**

Well, I would say whenever I feel like it. I will listen to some music when I feel tired or stressed at my work, it usually calms me down or makes me feel refreshed. I may even play some music when I feel it's too quiet in the house. It all depends.

- **Did you often listen to the music when you were a child?**

It's quite a long time ago, but I guess yes. I remember, as a kid, I was always very sensitive to music, my mom said I loved dancing to music whenever I heard any. I was also good at learning new songs. Apparently I could remember the melody very quickly.

- **Do you play any musical instrument?**

To be honest, I don't. I learnt to play the violin for a little bit but soon I gave it up. I thought it was boring and the sound of the violin was too jarring, almost scratchy. I regret now though, it could have been nice to be able to play an instrument.

- **Do you think it's necessary to offer a music course in high school?**

Yes, definitely. Music is good for cultural development and can also help children to develop their intelligence. According to scientific research, kids that are good at music are usually cleverer.

- **What is the influence of high tech on music?**

Well, it has put more possibilities and varieties into music. Although I don't know about the details, I heard that musicians now can use computer programs to help them compose and produce music.

- **Do you think songs composed through computer will replace those by musicians?**

I don't think so. Computer can help but not replace the musicians. Music is used to express our emotions, this is something that computers lack, it's just a machine, I don't think it will be able to produce something that can convey feelings.

Computer and internet

● Do you often use computers? What do you usually use computers for?

Yes, I do. I use it almost every day. A big part of it is for work, typing up documents, sending e-mails, searching for information online. etc. I sometimes do online reading or watching movies.

● What are the advantages and disadvantages of using computers?

I guess the biggest advantage is convenience. We can use computer for so many things now, such as contacting friends, finding information, enjoying all sorts of entertainment and working. The disadvantage is that many people rely too much on it or even become addicted to it. Some people even find it hard to live one day without the computer. I don't think we should let ourselves be controlled by it.

✓Joedy 点评：

口语和写作不一样，写作是结构精密的输出，所以非常讲究逻辑；而口语是直线型的输出，如果没有足够的把握，考生不要冒险去等分式地论证。也就是说，在口语表达时，应该尽量观点鲜明，直截了当，绝对不要模棱两可，东拉西扯。

像题目这样问the advantages and disadvantages of using computer，考生也不必真的是把使用电脑的所有优缺点都罗列出来。只需挑选一个最最重要的点说出来，然后重点论证这一点就OK了。记住，不求面面俱到，但求一点深入就好。

再来看看其他人是怎样看computer的。

Computer as I Know

Among all the great inventions created during the 20th century, there is no denying that computers are one of the most vital ones that have changed our life in an irreversible way.

Thanks to computers, our life is made more convenient and comfortable. We have easy access to information with the help of computer. Today, computers are fully exploited in every aspect of life: to do business control, medical care, to get education or to play games. Since all the people are connected through the internet, the world seems exactly small on the Internet where you can always exchange ideas with the people thousands of kilometers away in less than a few seconds.

Despite the very fact that our life has been greatly improved by

computer, we cannot turn a blind eye to the troubles it brings to us. It becomes increasingly disconcerting that people who spend all day playing with computer can easily get tired or even sick. People, especially the children are gradually losing the chances of enjoying the fresh air and bright sunshine because they have spent so much of their time in front of the screen playing games or doing some other things. What is worse is that computers, to some extent, block the communications among people. When everyone just sits in front of his computer, there is little time left for friend and family gatherings. In this case, computer is robbing our humanity.

It is tricky because computers have such advantages and disadvantages that people's opinions about it vary greatly. But it is the spirited discussion and emotional clashes triggered by computers that spice up our life so much. Believe it or not, computers have brought us into a new world we've never expected. It does improve our life though some troubles still exist.

Man is the greatest creature on this planet. I believe we're able to solve all the problems we meet. And I also believe that a harmonious rather than hostile relationship between human beings and computers can soon be achieved.

● What are good ways of learning computers?

I personally think that the best way is to try it. I learnt to use a computer by clicking every icon on the desktop then checked out what it was. It was quite good. I quickly got the hang of it. Maybe for some people, they would prefer to take some classes, which can also help.

● How do the elderly learn computers?

I think they mostly learn it through classes or the younger family members help them. We should not keep the elderly people away from the computers; instead, we should show them the benefits of using a computer or the internet and encourage them to learn it.

● When did you surf on the Internet for the first time?

Wow, that was long time ago. Let me see, as far as I can remember, it was the time when I got my first computer, it was a pretty crappy one, I was sixteen then. I didn't know anything about the Internet, I just wanted to try. I remember the first website I visited was Yahoo Mail. It took me a long time to register an e-mail address.

● Is the information on the Internet reliable?

I would say it depends. I always check out more websites if I read an important news. There have been so many reports about fake information and we should never just read it and believe it. But of course big famous websites are more reliable.

● How can people avoid false information?

It's difficult. That's why we should use our brain and analyze it. We can look up for more information to see how trustworthy it is. There are always loops in it if it's false.

● Do you like writing letters? Who do you write to the most?

No, I don't. I haven't hand-written any letters for a long time. I often write e-mails now. Mostly for work, I write to colleagues to ask about work or discuss about work related things.

● What type of letters are the most difficult one to write?

The question is a little bit vague. Formal letters maybe, because when I write formal letters, I need to be very careful with the way I address people, the tone I use, and carefully select the appropriate words and sentences. I can't be too casual.

● Which do you prefer, sending e-mails or writing letters?

I think not just for me, I guess for most people nowadays, sending e-mail is a preferred option. It's fast, convenient and cost almost nothing. However, I think the feeling of getting a real letter is totally different from that of getting an e-mail, even if the content is the same. I think somehow a real letter contains more things. It's a shame that we are so lazy now.

● Do you like to receive letters or phone calls?

Can I say I like both? I mean if they are from my friends, not from work. I can hear the voice through phone calls, it's vivid and intimate, but sometimes things are better described in written words.

✓Joedy 提示：

看看不同的联系方式以及他们的优缺点吧。

communicate face to face

benefits	challenges
direct interaction 直接的交流 less misunderstanding 少误会 focused 专注的	embarrassed 尴尬的 geographically limitations 地理局限 effortful 耗精力的

send / post a letter

benefits	challenges
warmth 温暖 traditional 传统的 original 原汁原味的	take time 花费时间 wasting trees 损耗木材 need to go to post office 去邮局寄

send an e-mail

benefits	challenges
attachment files can be sent 可发送附件 no stamps needed 不需要邮费 not limited to time 不受时间限制	attachments can contain viruses 附件可能包含病毒 cannot send physical objects 没法发送实物 unwanted junk e-mail 令人讨厌的垃圾邮件

make a phone call

benefits	challenges
convenient 方便的 handy for an emergency 在紧急关头派上用场 keep intimacy in spite of long distance 无论多远都可以保持紧密联系	radiation can cause headache and ear problems 辐射会造成头痛和耳朵问题 inappropriate use in public could be bothersome 公众场合不恰当使用会令人讨厌

create a blog / website

benefits	challenges
content can be updated anytime 可随时更新内容 a wide variety of content, including images, audio files, and animation is shared 可分享不同的信息例如图片，音频，动画等	can be time-consuming to maintain 维护很耗时间 feedback can be personal attacks 回复留言可能有人身攻击

use instant message	
benefits	challenges
interactive communication 互动式的交流 several people can participate simultaneously 可多人同时参与聊天 can see and hear each other when using Web cameras and microphones 可通过摄像头和麦克风看到彼此和听到彼此的声音	pose security risks 有隐私泄露隐患 People you want to chat with must be online when you are 聊天者必须同时在线

Shopping

● Do you like shopping?

No, I don't. It may sound strange for a woman, but I really don't like wandering in shopping malls. It's too crowded and I find it a waste of time. I only go shopping if I have a clear target. I just get there, buy it and go.

● When do you go shopping?

I only go when there's a need for something, mostly grocery shopping after work. Sometimes at weekends, I will go shopping for the things I need, but I never spend too much time on it.

● Which kind of things do you like to buy?

It's hard to say, things I need, such as food, clothes and shoes. There's something particular I like to buy, which is books. I like spending hours in bookshops searching for books I like.

● What kinds of shops do you like going to?

I like going to supermarkets because there I can finish my grocery shopping in one go. For clothes and shoes, I prefer to go to small shops, they usually have more interesting and unique designs than the franchised ones.

● Which is your favorite way of shopping?

I think it's online shopping, because it can save me a lot of time and I don't need to join the shopping crowds out there. However, it's just the beginning here in China, the regulations are not complete yet and there is a possibility that you don't get what you see online.

● Can you recommend a good shop for foreign visitors to Guangzhou?

There are really a lot of shops in Guangzhou, it's not easy to come up with one now, let me see… If the foreigners want to buy traditional Cantonese things, I would suggest that they should go to the Shangxiajiu shopping street or the side streets near there, there are a lot of local shops for the foreigners to discover. If they just want to buy daily things, they can go to Teemall or China Plaza, they have everything they need I think.

● Are the shops the same to the shops decades ago?

I think the shops are very different now. I remember when I was a little girl, there was nothing like supermarket or shopping mall, we always had to ask the shop assistant to bring what we want to buy over the counter, no direct access to the products for the customers. Nowadays the layout in the shop is completely transformed; we can look at and touch whatever we are interested in easily.

● Is shopping very important to people? Why?

For most people it's important I guess. It's the most popular pastime all over the world. People have to buy what they need for their life, grocery shopping, for example. But I don't think people should spend too much time or money on it, consumerism is unhealthy.

Sports

● How do you keep fit and healthy? What sports do you usually do?

To be honest, I am now quite lazy and I don't do sports very often, but I do try to eat healthily, I make sure I eat a lot of vegetable and fruits. I used to swim a lot and bike a lot on my home-trainer, now the sport I do most frequently is maybe climbing the stairs when I go home every day, still a kind of sport, I assume.

● What is the most popular sport in your country?

I think it's table tennis, it's our national sport, which doesn't mean that I can play it well though. You know, our athletes always get all the gold medals in the Olympics, many people especially the young kids are influenced and encouraged by it, so they like to practice playing it. It's also because it doesn't need a lot of space or equipment. I see people playing it in my community quite often.

● **Which kind of sports do people in your hometown like?**

People in Guangzhou like swimming very much, I think it's because of the climate here, we have very hot and long summer. Being in the swimming pool is a great pleasure, plus it's cheap to go swimming here.

● **Which is the most important sport in China?**

There are many, badminton, table tennis, swimming, platform diving, volleyball and so on. I can't say there's just one most important sport.

● **Do you think children should learn sports at school?**

Absolutely, I even think that the Chinese schools should provide more PE classes to the kids. Physical development is important for school kids, they need a healthy body for study and for their life, but many parents and teachers are ignoring this fact.

✓ **Joedy 点评：**

2009年这一场"猪流感"弄得大家人心惶惶，"健康"概念又显得重要起来了。人们除了要饮食健康还要有适当的运动，那运动除了给人们带来健康之外，还带来什么呢？运动对孩子到底有什么benefits呢？

看看我从http://www.buzzle.com摘下的文章：

Benefits of Playing Sports

Playing sports is one of the favorite activities of most of us. Apart from being a fun activity, sports offer several health benefits, thus contributing to one's physical and mental well-being. Sports play a vital role in the enhancement of one's personality by being a source of exercise and entertainment. Let us look at the benefits of playing sports.

Sports serve as an excellent physical exercise. Those who play sports have a more positive body image than those who do not. Playing sports often involves physical activities like running, jumping and stretching and moreover a constructive expenditure of energy. Playing sports since an early age strengthens the bones and muscles and tones one's body. Thus sports provide the body with a complete exercise.

Playing sports improves the Math skills in children. It develops leadership qualities and fosters a team spirit in them. Sports involve competition, they involve winning and losing. This exposes the players to both the aspects of life, successes and failures. Sports build a competitive spirit in children and teach them to be participative irrespective of whether the participation concludes in a victory or a defeat. Playing sports teaches a person to accept both successes and failures in a positive spirit. The most important benefit of playing sports is the sportsman spirit. Playing sports results in the development of a sportive nature, which is helpful throughout one's life.

Playing sports is very beneficial for the development of social skills in a person. Sports teach a person to interact with people, act as a team. They foster collective thinking and develop planning skills in children. Sports build confidence in children and give them a sense of accomplishment. Sports thus play a vital role in one's social well-being.

Playing sports requires the children to plan thoughtfully. They need to device the best ways to score goals, the best strategies to win and plan carefully towards victory. Statistics show that kids involved in sports activities fare well in academics and their school and college activities.

A constructive expenditure of energy that sports bring out is very helpful in keeping a person happy. Exercise generates happiness molecules in a person's body, thus contributing to his/her mental well-being. Sports generate a positive energy.

Playing sports serves as an excellent exercise, which has a wide variety of health benefits. It reduces blood sugar level and reduces the risk of blood cholesterol. Playing sports decreases the chances of hypertension and several other stress related disorders. Research has revealed that people who play sports regularly can deal with stresses and strains in life in a better manner. Depression, anxiety and other psychological disorders are less probable in people who indulge in sport activities.

Regular exercise helps increase the overall quality of life. Playing sports acts as a beautiful blend of recreation and physical activity. It is a combination of both enjoyment and exercise.

● What is the difference between the sports boys do and those girls do?

I think boys are more into competitive and contact sports, such as basketball, football, martial arts, because they like to feel the power and strength they have. While the girls prefer gentle sports, like dancing, gymnastics, yoga, these sports help to show the beauty of their body.

✓Joedy 点评：

Sports特别是team sports对孩子的身心有很大益处。雅思口语考题中经常会让考生作比较，而"个人与集体"是其中一种重要的比较。现在来看看team sports有什么benefits吧。

The Benefits of Team Sports for Children

While the opinion that children can benefit physically from participating in team sports, little attention, if there is any, has been drawn to the psychological benefits associated with encouraging their children to get involved in team sports that they enjoy. The great importance of physical activities is widely  acknowledged due to the fact that many of our children are now overweight. Studies show that currently, only one out of four adolescent children participated in any type of organized physical activity on a regular basis, which, by all means, has something to do with the increasing number of obese adolescents in America.

As is known to all, exercise is very beneficial when it comes to both the physical and the mental well being in participants. People in sports teams burn calories by exercising, helping to ward off any weight problems that may be present. Exercise is also known as a low-risk therapy healing metal problems such as insomnia, depression, and low self-esteem, which is important in the world of today where many children feel inadequate due to all the perfection displayed in the virtual world created by the media and the Internet. Regular physical activity also helps the body to manage stress, ensuring a physically fit individual of an optimistic and calm attitude, which can help them to get through stressful times without difficulty. A study conducted by the Women's Sports Foundation revealed that adolescents that were regularly involved in team sports were less likely to engage in sexual activity until later in life than those who were not in team sports. Also, teens on sport teams were found to be less likely to use drugs than their non-playing counterparts. In addition, the students involved in sports had a higher chance of graduating from high school and college.

 The benefits and rewards associated with setting goals and following through on a sports team are innumerable, and for this very reason, it is necessary for adults to enroll their children on some type of team sport. While there are various types of sports for children to take part in, which specific type should be chosen simply does not matter, as just being on the team and physically exerting themselves can give your children a healthier life.

✓Joedy 点评：

　　划线的部分是大家可以在考试当中用上的地道词组搭配，特别是在提及身心健康方面的问题的时候特别有用。

● **Do you like swimming? Where can you swim near your home?**

Yes, I do. I love swimming. I was in the swimming team when I was in middle school, I like being in the pool, it's cool and relaxing. There are a few swimming pools within my community, so it's quite easy for me to go jump into the pool.

● **Is swimming a popular sport in your country?**

I guess so, it's not an expensive sport and it's very good for our body. Most of my family members and friends can swim, and I see swimming pools and water parks in cities a lot.

● **What benefits can swimming bring to people?**

Swimming is considered to be the best sport for our body. It has scientific ground. People do not need to bear any pressure when they are floating in water, and there's not as much impact on our joints, not like running or playing tennis. Swimming also helps with our body balance and reduces stress.

Weekend

● **What do you usually do at weekends?**

I basically relax at weekends. I like sleeping in, and then will think about what to do, never have any clear plans. I sometimes go shopping, sometimes meet up with friends, sometimes go on day trips.

● **Where do you usually go at weekends?**

It depends. If I want to go shopping, I go to shopping malls or supermarkets, if I want to watch movies, I'll go to the cinema, or maybe I go on day trips to the neighboring cities.

● **Some people do part-time job at weekends. Do you agree?**

I guess it's a personal choice. I have no problem with that. I will not do it myself though, I need time to relax and reload my energy battery for the new week. Working seven days a week for more money is definitely not an option for me.

● **Do you think it acceptable that the employers have the employees work at weekends?**

I will still say it's a personal choice. Whether it is acceptable or not all depends on how you look at it, some people prefer to work to get extra money, so they will be more than happy to take the employers' offer. But employees should have the right to say no if they don't want to do it, it would be unacceptable if the employer blames them for saying no.

● **Do you think the employees will accept working at weekends?**

It depends, if the company provides lucrative benefits, probably many employees will accept working at weekends, but of course some people will still prefer to have time off to relax and to spend time with family and friends. It's up to the need of the individuals.

Holidays and traveling

● **When was your last holiday?**

It was in April, I had a five-day holiday. I went on a trip to Xiamen, had a very nice and relaxing time there, visited some attractions and tasted a lot of local food.

● **What do you like or hate to do in holidays?**

I like flying to a different city and doing things there without planning, or maybe just being there and doing nothing, simply strolling around and seeing what I can discover. The part I don't like about a holiday is when I need to come back, because I don't want it to end!

● **What do people do in Chinese festivals?**

They do things according to the traditions, for example, on Mid-autumn Festival people will eat moon cakes, on dragon boat festival people will eat rice cake and watch dragon boat race, on Spring Festival people will play with firecrackers and give lucky money. What's in common is that people will always spend time with their family no matter which festival they are having.

● **Do people send presents in holidays? Is holiday important?**

Yes, we do. But it's not necessary. Holidays are important because people get time to relax and be with their family, and traditional holidays help us to keep our customs and traditions.

● **Do you think there should be more holidays in the future?**

Yes, the more the better. I think Chinese people have a ridiculously small amount of holidays comparing to other countries. For example, we only have seven days during the Spring Festival, which is our most important festival. Seven days is definitely not enough, you can't do much within such a short period of time. The students and the working people both need more holidays to relax.

● Do you like traveling?

Yes, I do. I love traveling. Traveling not only gives me a chance to relax, it also provides me an opportunity to experience different cultures and visit new places.

● Do you like going traveling alone or with friends?

I prefer to go traveling alone, I don't like big groups, there's always so much more to consider when you are traveling with a group, sometimes it takes ages before we can agree on doing something. I think traveling alone is freer, and I can also make new friends on my trip.

● What problems will people encounter during the journey?

So far I haven't had any problems on my trip. I guess finding the right transportation can be difficult sometimes, especially when you are in a small town. Food can be another one, people may not be used to the taste of local food. For example, if you go to Sichuan and you can not eat spicy food, you probably will have to eat crackers for a while.

● What should be taken into consideration when traveling abroad?

Perhaps people should read something about the place they are going to visit, just to get a gist of the culture there, and maybe people can try to learn some basic expressions in that language, so they can use it when they are in some situation. Of course, we can also check out the weather there, and then we can prepare the clothes we need.

● Do you think tourism has a bad effect on the local people?

Every coin has two sides. I can't say tourism only has negative effects on the local people; it definitely brings job opportunities and money there. However, it may also spoil the tranquility and the local environment. It will also bring pollution if the tourists don't take the responsibility of keeping the place clean.

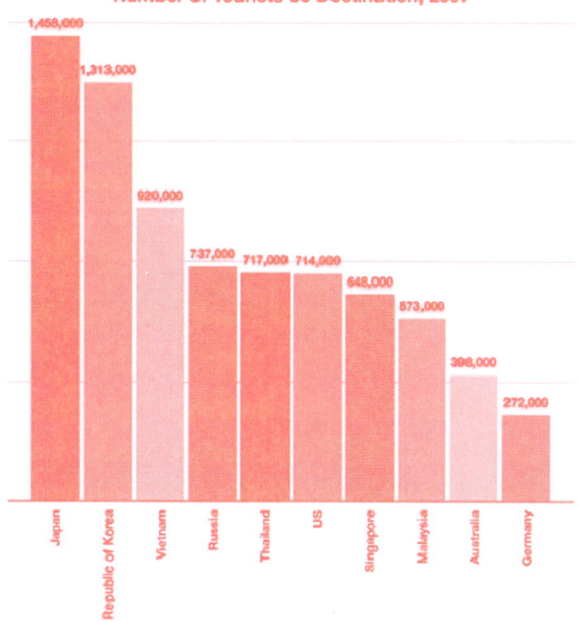

Art and museum / art gallery

● Which is your favorite form of art, such as painting and sculpture?

In fact, I am not very into art. I can see if a painting or a sculpture is beautiful or not, but I can't make profound judgment on it. I don't really have a preference over these two forms of art.

✓Joedy 点评：

很多考生对于art这个概念非常模糊，觉得art是个很抽象的概念。到底什么是art？art又大略分成多少种呢？看看国外的网友怎么说。

What kind of Art Are You Interested in?

I'm into painting, photography, drawing, digital drawing and manipulation. Also I'm studying Graphic Design for my major!

I love abstract art and creative writing. I have half a book finished but my last chapter got stuck on my CD where I saved it all. So I haven't been able to finish it. I also like poetry. For photography, I just think it's truly amazing how we can <u>capture the world and life in such ways</u>. The pictures don't lie unless altered by photoshop haha.

✓Joedy 点评：

喜欢摄影的考生要注意划线部分的表达了，表示摄影捕捉美丽的瞬间，考生还可以这样描述：Photography is the only way that we are able to capture the genuine beauty of the world as well as the memorable moments in our life.

I'm old-fashioned in the sense that I love classic-style drawing and painting... I can't draw for the life of me, so I've always been jealous of those who can! I also enjoy the performing arts — I love going to see plays and musicals. Some other forms of art that I'm really into are: basket weaving (or just weaving in general), glass-blowing, pottery, and sculpted art.

✓Joedy 点评：

划线部分是考生不容易想到的观点，记住，在考试的时候，个性化的观点往往能够帮助考生脱颖而出。

Music is just a way to describe anything, whether you are sad or happy or just content with the way life is going. Listening to a specific song can change your mood. Listening to a song in the morning can alter the way you look at that day. Music is just a way to express yourself.

I am really into drawing, scrap-booking, poetry, and ceramics. I also love to watch performances, but if I am involved with one, I tend to work more behind-the-scenes. I am good at drawing nature more than people. I am a beginner at ceramics because I cannot yet work out the pottery wheel.

I love contemporary art, illustration and photography (especially love Man Ray's work and historical photos). If I had enough money to get my own place, I would choose use Japanese and Swedish (not Ikea) design elements. I love them for how clean, minimalist and functional they are. I also like to see sewing and fashion as art. I was in heaven when I worked briefly in theater costuming, but alas, the hours were too long and the pay was not great.

✓Joedy 点评：

正如划线部分一样，大家会发现native speakers讲话都很夸张。但是如果能够在用英语交流的时候学会适当地使用类似的夸张表达，可以令大家的讲话更加生动和富有感染力。

Dance is pretty cool. I love clogging. It's seriously the coolest dance ever. Not very known in America, but I really like it. Music and dance are definitely the arts that I'm into right now. I do want to know more about painting and artist like Da Vinci, Monet. I'm reading Da Vinci Code and the character Robert Langdon makes are seem to be so precious and valuable, which makes me want to know about it and learn more.

Photography is my thing, but it must be film. I am not into the digital world. I have used the same 35mm Nikon for twelve years and I doubt I will ever give it up. It is my medium of choice. My dad is a professional photographer and he taught me most of what I know. He shoots weddings, portraits and runway shows.

✓Joedy 点评：

考生在雅思口语考试当中常常会被问到关于个人喜好的问题，但是很多考生都只使用最简单的表达，例如：I like...等。到目前为止，我在这本书里面提供了各种各样的表达喜好的方法，大家现在开始整理吧。不仅仅是这篇文章提到的I am really into...或者...is my thing。

● What is the significance and value of art?

I think it can educate people and it can develop our sense for beauty.

✓Joedy 点评：

好了，从上面大家的讨论中，大家对art的种类略知一二了吧。那么art有什么意义和价值呢？

What is the Significance of Art

Art is such a simple term but it is difficult to define. To a child, art is drawing and coloring. For celebrities, art is acting and entertaining. For designers, art is trend and fashion. The definition of art can be very objective.

Different sectors have their own definition of art. They have various standards too. For a mother, the drawings of her children are works of art. For museums, art is the genuine creation of a significant artist in the past.

Just like its definition, its significance also varies. There are various forms of art today, and each is important to the artist involved. A good example is a musician. Music is a good example of art. That is why singers are called artists. For a songwriter, each song has a story that he wants the people to hear. For most writers, this is very personal.

For various artists, art is a way of expressing themselves. You may have seen an abstract oil painting, although you cannot recognize the patterns and strokes of the artists, it is very important for the painter. For him, it represents his emotion and his character. It can symbolize his anger and frustration. However, it can also represent his love and compassion. Anyone who sees it can also use it to represent how they feel. Strokes and colors can evoke certain emotions from other people. This is why most people want to buy pieces of artwork.

For others, it represents their dreams. The television today has produced several competitions that opened the doors for various dreamers. There are dancers across the country who lined up to audition because all their life they wanted to dance in front of an audience who appreciates what they can do. Many have gone to school to enhance their skills so that they can be among the best dancers in the world.

Like music, dancing is a form of art that can evoke various feelings. <u>Aside from love, dances can also evoke sensuality, excitement, fun, passion, anger, and happiness.</u> Art here is more than entertainment and talent. It is more of touching people's life through their moves and choreography.

<u>Today, art also symbolizes comfort.</u> You can see art in many beautiful and comfortable homes. Interior designers are also artists in many ways. They match things to provide a wonderful space for their clients. Seeing the overwhelming reactions of their clients gives them satisfaction. To them, that is the most rewarding feeling.

<u>Art has also transcended in foods.</u> Many cooks and chefs have proven this. Some may be predictable but others are like the abstract oil painting. You do not care what is in there as long as you like the taste. For them, being able to feed and satisfy their customers is all that matters.

Art is very significant in today's generation. Since it has taken various forms, it has earned the respect of almost all the artists. Musicians respect their instruments, painters respect their brushes, paints, and canvass, and chefs respect their ingredients and utensils.

Art is significant because of the sense of fulfillment an artist feels every time he finishes a masterpiece.

● Did you learn any form of art when you were a child?

Yes, I did. I learnt drawing for a few years. As a kid, I liked drawing random things on paper, my mom saw it and she sent me to the drawing classes, but I gave it up later as I got too busy with my study.

● How do Chinese appreciate art from other countries?

I think we keep a learning attitude on that, Chinese people try to learn the good things from the foreign art and then fit it into our own culture and develop it.

● Would you like to visit a museum to enjoy art?

Sometimes. I have been to an art museum a couple times, mainly out of curiosity when I see an ad.. I must admit that I don't always understand it, especially the modern art or post-modern art.

● Did you ever go to the museum or art gallery when you were a child?

I really don't remember. That's too long ago. I for sure visited some museums, to learn history, but an art gallery, probably not.

● Tell me an experience that you had when you went to the museum or art gallery.

I remember the time when I went to the Macau museum. It was last month, it was not a very big museum but neat and well-organized. There are three floors, on the first floor they display the history of Macau and how it became the Portuguese colony, then the second floor is the local customs and traditions of Macau, I like that floor the best, because GZ and Macau share the same kind of customs and traditions, I could relate a lot things that I know to the displayed items. It was a pity that the third floor was under construction, or I could have seen more things.

● What do you think you can learn from visiting museums and galleries?

A lot! When you visit a history museum, you can learn a lot of things that happened in the past, for example, when I go to the Forbidden City, I learned many things about the Qing Dynasty. When you visit the art museum, you learn about the development of arts and can see a lot of either real or replicas of famous arts.

● What roles do museums play in a city?

Educate and preserve history or culture. A museum is a place that people can learn a lot of different things, it also has the responsibility to preserve cultural or historical things, it needs to keep the display items in good shape so that more and more people can see them.

● What should be done to attract more visitors to museums and galleries?

The best way, I would say, is to make it free. People will be more willing to visit if there's no entrance fee, and they should also hold themed exhibitions regularly instead of just exhibiting the same things all the time, then people who are interested in specific themes can go and it will not be so boring.

Reading

● Do you like reading? What books do you usually read? Why?

Yes, I do. I read quite a lot. I like reading history books because I am interested in the ancient development of the society, there are a lot of things to learn from the ancient wisdom too.

● Do you like reading academic books?

Not really, I only read academic books when I have to, like for my job or writing an essay. They are usually very complicated and specialized in certain fields, not for leisure reading.

● Why do some people not like reading?

I am not sure about that, because I like reading and I find pleasure in it. I guess those who don't enjoy reading are not interested in learning new things or they would rather do something they think is more interesting.

● Did you read any books when you were a child?

Yes, I did. I read a lot of fairytales, the Anderson's, the Green Brothers', Chinese fairytales. I often asked my mom to buy me books, through which I also learnt a lot of new characters even before I went to primary school.

● Do you think children in China nowadays like reading?

No, I don't think so. Too much of their attention has been diverted to TV and computer games, they think those are more exciting. And I think schools are not encouraging them to read anything but text books.

● What books do children like reading now?

I think most of them like to read comic books, especially the Japanese ones, the older kids like to read fantasy books or romantic novels.

● What influence does reading have on children?

Books broaden their horizons and enrich their knowledge, if they read the right ones. That's why I think parents should help them choose books; kids may get wrong things from inappropriate books.

✓Joedy 点评：

先总体来看看reading的好处。其实，reading作为"爱好"的一种，对人们所产生的影响和其他的爱好都一样，无非是对"身心"的影响嘛！

What are the benefits from reading?

Few people, if there are any, can deny the fact that reading helps us to enhance our life in a mental and social way. Also, if we develop a habit of reading, our ability to comprehend all sorts of information as well as our confidence in doing so can be strengthened. Let's explore other benefits of reading in great details.

One of the other main benefits of reading is that it exercises your mind. Your mind begins to bend and flex mentally, making itself lose and limber to flow easier during the day. The regular reading habit ensures that the reading muscle as well as the mind stay in good shape.

Reading enhances people's ability to focus. When the mind is trained up by the action of reading, it begins to pay attention more thoroughly. In other words, the more you read, the longer time you can stay focused. Therefore, when you are faced with some of life's difficult and challenging assignments, you, compared with those who seldom read, will have greater ability to stay calm and deal with the problems or the required task in an objective way.

There is perhaps no greater avenue to learning than through reading. All people, regardless of their age, professions and social status, have learned more things by reading than practically anywhere other way. When we continue to read, we have the ability to expand our minds tremendously. We review the pages of knowledge left by those who came before us, which is of significant meanings because books are the priceless collection of human wisdom. We then begin to add to the knowledge, again leaving the invisible yet powerful treasure for those who come after us, which is how the cycle of human civilization continues.

Finally, when we conduct a practice of reading, we are building solid foundation for our future academic study. This foundation of reading will also allow us to realize many goals and ambitions we have for our lives. Our habit of continuing to read helps to ensure we will continue to succeed.

✓Joedy 点评：

以上是关于reading的好处都可以应用到其他的爱好类，例如：painting, dancing, watching TV and movies等等。大家要学会举一反三。

再看看两个网友的说法。

It gives you different points of view to the world and broadens your vocabulary. And I know from personal experience that it can take you to another world of happiness or whatever is going on in that book. It gives you a sense of stability when things aren't going so well in your life, because things never change in the book. And there are always different types of books from a variety of different authors who have a different type of style that can suite your mind, personality, emotions, and imagination and even your creativity. Books can inspire you!

If you read a novel, you can experience what it would be like to be that person. So, through novels you can have dozens of different lives to the one you have now! How's that for broadening your mind? Non-fiction books can give you information and that means you can check up on what people tell you, to get to the truth. They say the truth will set you free.

Daily routines

● What is your daily routine?

Usually I get up at eight, have breakfast at home then I go to work, I work until six, then go home and cook, after that, I will watch some TV or do some reading. I normally don't go out in the evening, too tired after work. I usually go to bed around eleven.

● What time do you usually get up?

On the weekdays, I get up at 8, at the weekends, I always sleep in, sometimes I may get up at noon, sleeping in is the luxury I want to enjoy the most at the weekend.

● **What do you usually do in the evening?**

Nothing special, most of the time I just stay at home, either watch movies or read, I don't like going out to drink or socialize. I sometimes meet up with my friends for dinner.

● **Do you follow the same routine every night?**

Pretty much yes, unless there are some special arrangements or important things to do. Maybe it sounds boring, but it's the truth.

● **Was your nightlife the same as that of now?**

Nightlife? I never had any nightlife, when I was a student, I spent my evenings doing homework and studying, now I am working, I go home after work. I don't like going to pubs or anything like that at night.

● **Where do you like to go in the evening?**

I like going home in the evening. If I go out, I usually go to take a walk within my neighborhood, or maybe eat out, I don't stay out late.

● **Is there any difference between your routine now and in your childhood?**

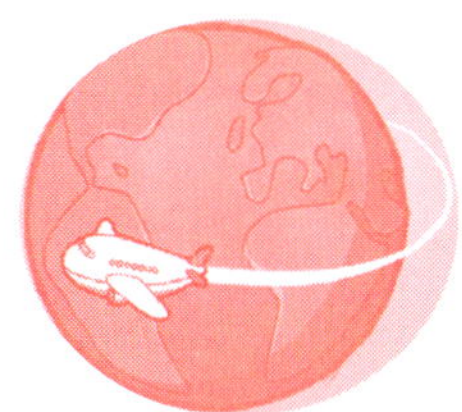

Yes, there is. I go to bed a lot later now; I used to sleep more as a child. I didn't work, I studied. That's the biggest difference.

● **What time in a day do you like best?**

My favorite period of time in a day is late afternoon, just before sun set, because on my way home, when I pass the houses, I always smell the cooking from different homes; see the I-want-to-go-home expression on everybody's face and the beautiful sunset. All that gives me a very homey and heart-warming feeling.

● **How would you like to change your life?**

At the moment, I am pretty happy with my life, there's nothing I want to change. If I have to come up with something, I would say I had dreamt about traveling around the world, I would love to be a full-time traveler. It's not easy, and it takes time to make enough money for that.

● **Will you change your routines as the four seasons changing?**

Not really. First of all, there are no distinct seasons in my city, I don't need to think about changing my routines for that, I may go to bed earlier in winter because it's cozy in bed when it's cold.

Lesson 3 Part 2 审题训练与真题讲解

★ Cue card审题训练

> Describe a leisure activity that keeps you healthy (the healthy life-style).
>
> You should say:
>
> > What it is.
> >
> > How you got to know this way.
> >
> > How and when it turn to be important.
> >
> > How often you keep healthy in this way.
>
> And explain the reason why you think it is good for keeping healthy.

✓ **Joedy** 提醒：

　　这一张卡片主要是讲"一种保持身体健康的方式"，有些考生会讲 sleeping, thinking, reading等等，这些的确是属于"帮助身心健康的休闲活动"。但是建议大家还是准备一个"运动"会比较好，这样比较方便转题。近年来健康是个很重要的话题，而运动保持健康是雅思口语考试常涉及到的，例如有时考生会被要求讲"an exciting sport you like"，有时也会让考生讲"an outdoor activity"，如果大家准备的是sleeping, thinking之类的，就有很大局限性了。好了，现在大家来想想讲什么比较好。

★ Cue card真题点评与参考答案

My topic is about a leisure activity that keeps me healthy. I think for me that's swimming. I learnt swimming when I was five, my father taught me. He taught me because he said it's a very important life skill. It took me quite a while to learn it because at the beginning I was afraid of water, I wanted to give up. My father insisted and he gave me a lot of patience. Slowly I became good at it and I was chosen to be a swimming team member. Ever since then, I have loved being in water. I think swimming has also helped me grow taller. I keep this habit up. Now I go swimming twice a week, usually in the evening or at weekend. I always feel very free and relaxed when I am in the pool, I don't need to think about anything but enjoy the coolness of the water. Every time I go swimming I make sure I swim no less than 800 meters. I think swimming is the best sport for my body because when I swim, I don't feel any pressure on any parts of my body, and every part of my body is exercised. And actually I sweat a lot and I burn a lot of calories, but I will not have the annoying sticky feeling like when I do other sports. Plus it's a sport that I don't need to look for any partner, I can go whenever I like. That's why I choose swimming as my favorite leisure activity.

✓Joedy 点评：

这个leisure activity一旦准备好，大家就可以转化成许多热门的卡片了，例如：

Your favorite magazine / newspaper / website，考生就可以讲关于这个leisure activity的报刊、杂志或者网站）；如果是an interesting speech / lesson呢？考生也可以说是关于这种休闲活动的讲座；还可以转成a course you would like to take in the future，大家只需要改头换面就可以了。最重要的是要胆大心细。

好了，现在再提供一个native speaker的答案给大家，非常地道的口语。希望对大家开拓思路有帮助。

I love sports — they're one of the reasons why I actually like going to school. I'm on the varsity swimming, volleyball, and badminton teams. I was going to try out for soccer, but I have a knack of getting injured (I sprained my ankle tripping on a slide once) so my parents didn't want me to. I was going to go for basketball, but it isn't really my sport. I love playing it during lunch time and after school, but I can never imagine myself playing it competitively.

We don't have a tennis, netball, rugby, or football team at my school, which really sucks, because I would love to play them. My dad is a tennis freak and is part of the city team. I used to practice every weekend, but when I ended up injuring many of my trainers (including sending one to the doctor because I swung really hard, and the ball smacked him on the forehead).

I love sports with all my heart, but I have big issue with getting injured... and injuring people in the process. But it's all good because it's totally worth it. It's exhilarating to play the sport that you love.

✓Joedy 提醒：

"爱好"这个话题几乎是交流场合中不可缺少的一部分，爱好的类型有好多，常见的有 doing sports, traveling, surfing the Internet, reading等等。常见的思路有：

1. How you got to know about it?

2. How you do it?

3. What influence on you?

谈到为什么喜欢上这个爱好，大家应尽量解释充分一点，最好就是强调此爱好对自己身心带来的影响的整个过程，大家可以像讲故事一样，谈到此爱好如何帮助自己gain knowledge，也可以提到此爱好如何让自己变得更加relaxed and think more clearly的，更可以提到此爱好如何让自己走出isolation，变得更加communicative的。总之，多强调此爱好对自己身体和心灵上的帮助就好啦。

Lesson 4 Part 3 听题训练

✓Joedy 提醒：

Hobbies这个话题到了Part 3其实问题和很多Part 1的很相像，只是问题的广度和深度有所提升，很自然，考官使用的词语与句型也相对更复杂一点。所以大家听题目的时候要打起十二分精神，不要慌神！好好开声读以下的题目吧。

Health

- Do you think health is important to people? Why?

- What did people do to keep their bodies fit in the past?

- What changes do people need to make their life healthier?

- Is it the responsibilities for the media to teach people how to keep healthy?

- Are doctors responsible for teaching people how to keep healthy?

- Can parents give children advice on how to keep healthy?

- Why are some people reluctant to follow the ways of keeping good health even though they know how to do it?

- What should the school do to help students to become healthier?

- What do you think of the people who smoke cigarettes in your country?

- What should the government do to cope with the smoking problem?

<table>
<tr><td align="center">Music</td></tr>
</table>

- What different music do people at different ages like?

- What are the benefits of listening to the music for children?

- What different music do people listen to in different situations?

- What is the influence of western music on Chinese music?

- What is the music like in the shopping mall and in the supermarket?

Art and museum / art gallery

- Do Chinese people like appreciating art?
- Why do you think some people spend a fortune on artworks and put it at home?
- Where do you usually go for enjoying art?
- Are there any art galleries in your hometown?
- Is it important for people to go to the art gallery?
- What are the different attitudes towards art between young and old?
- What different artworks do the young and the elderly like?
- What type of Chinese traditional arts is popular?
- Do you think the advertisement is a form of arts?
- What are the differences between well-made objects and art?
- What are the differences between the Chinese art works and western ones?
- Do teenagers like foreign artworks?
- Do you think artists are being well paid nowadays?
- What should the government do to protect the art?
- Should the government invest more money on art?

<table>
<tr><td align="center">Reading</td></tr>
</table>

- What kinds of books are popular among children now?

- What kinds of books are suitable for children?

- Is reading important for children?

- Which is better, books or TV?

- Do children in China like reading?

- Will e-books replace traditional books in the future?

- What should parents do in order to arouse children's interest in reading?

- Are teachers playing a more important role in guiding children?

- How is the Internet used in libraries?

- How can more people be attracted to libraries?

- How will libraries in the future be like?

Lesson 5 Part 3 真题讲解与参考答案

Health

● **Do you think health is important to people? Why?**

It's crucial to us. If we are not healthy or sick, we can't do anything. We will not be able to work or study normally; we will not even be able to enjoy our life the way we want to, for example, if I am sick, I can't go traveling. Being unhealthy can also be very costly, so costly that we can not afford it, it's very expensive to go to hospital in China, we can't afford to be sick.

I think also by doing sports. It seems to me that the older generations are healthier than the younger ones, although we are supposed to have better nutrition and more advanced health care nowadays. I think people in the past did more manual work and moved more than us, working meant exercise to them. Also things they eat might be more primitive, but at the same time, less additives in it, we are swallowing too any chemicals nowadays.

● What changes do people need to make their life healthier?

For the modern people, the first thing they need to do is to get off their chair in front of the TV or computer, go out and do some exercises. We should also keep a healthy diet; eat more veggies and fruits, less junk food like KFC or Mcdonald's. People should not drink or smoke. Of course people should also learn to retreat from their work, get some time to relax and travel, that's also very important for our mental health.

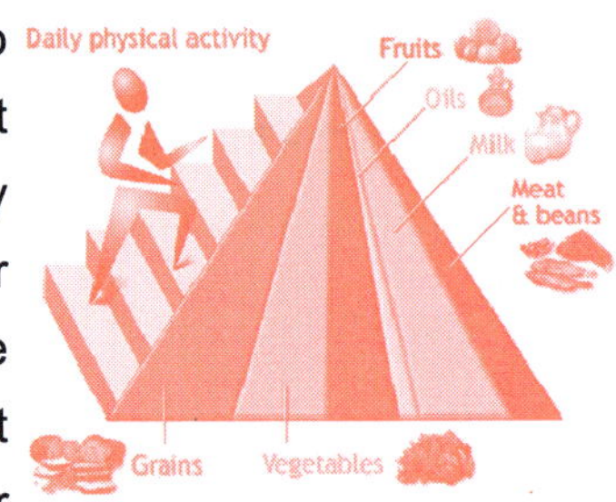

● Is it the responsibilities for the media to teach people how to keep healthy?

Yes, absolutely. Nowadays the media has enormous influence on our society, if they don't convey the right thing, it can be very harmful. If every day the fast food commercials are shown on TV and telling people how tasty they are, people will be misled and go to eat it. The media should encourage people to do things that help keep them healthy, such as eating the right thing and doing sports.

● Are doctors responsible for teaching people how to keep healthy?

Yes, doctors can help, but it's still up to the individuals. Doctors can give professional advice to people and give them guidance on how to stay healthy. They can also help people analyze their health condition and give them specific suggestions.

● Can parents give children advice on how to keep healthy?

Yes, I think parents have the responsibility to keep their children healthy, especially the younger ones. Parents should be the children's role models; they need to have a healthy life style themselves. They also need to help the kids select the right things to eat and do exercises together with them.

● Why are some people reluctant to follow the ways of keeping good health even though they know how to do it?

Probably they are too weak, and they try to block the fact that they are eating something bad when they do so. Or maybe they don't care, they don't want to be responsible for their own health, it can also be that they don't feel the negative effect on their body immediately so they think it doesn't matter. That is very stupid though.

● What should the school do to help students to become healthier?

The schools in China should give more time to the kids to do sports, they also need to give less homework. The schools here just care about academic things, the teachers should really care more about the students' healthy life. They should give classes on nutrition and physical health.

● What do you think of the people who smoke cigarettes in your country?

They are one bunch of selfish people. They are killing themselves and also killing other innocent people. Every day we take in so much second-hand smoke, they are just polluting the public places, I really think we should strictly ban public smoking.

● What should the government do to cope with the smoking problem?

Although it doesn't really help, government should still force the tobacco companies to print warnings on the package. The government should also charge incredibly high tax on cigarettes, then most people will have to smoke less, smoking in China is way too cheap. The government should ban public smoking and make it inconvenient for people to smoke.

Music

● **What different music do people at different ages like?**

Young people like fast, noisy and exciting music like pop music, hip-hop, hard rock and so on, while the older people prefer classical, opera, more traditional kind of music.

● **What are the benefits of listening to music for children?**

Music can make children more intelligent, kids that are good at musical instruments are usually very smart, although it doesn't necessarily show in their studies, it shows in other ways in their life. Music can also help children calm down and have better concentration. Scientists said that kids learn better after they listen to some music.

● **What different music do people listen to in different situations?**

When people are stressed, music can help them relax. When people are in a happy situation, music can bring the happiness to a higher level, like people always use some music at festivals or on special occasions like parties. Music is a very special ingredient in our life.

● **What is the influence of western music on Chinese music?**

To be honest, I don't know very much about that. I think Chinese musicians take the essence of western music and melt it into the making of Chinese music. They also learn things from it.

✓ Joedy 点评：

在Part 3的"对比类"题型中，"East VS West"是其中一类对比。来看看Chinese traditional music的变化吧。

One of the most vital characteristics of all cultures — Music. The Music of China is truly one-of-a-kind. When listening to Chinese music, those who are not familiar with it will know that what they're hearing is something very different and truly breathtaking. Even modern Chinese music, in a style very much like Western modern music, is somewhat distinct.

Why is this so? Why does Chinese music sound different from Western music? Traditional Chinese music puts certain emphasis on each of the five musical elements much differently than its Western counterpart. Chinese music also uses a different scale, using a five-tone scale rather than the eight-tone scale of Western music. One cannot also ignore the fact that

Chinese music is sung in the Chinese language, which will surprise and strike many Westerners as odd and incredible.

Although different and seemingly "odd", Chinese Music is unique and beautiful in its own and special way. So open up those ears and speakers, and get ready for a Chinese musical treat!

Instruments

The traditional Chinese instruments of China — producing beautiful sounds and enchanting melodies.

Traditional Chinese Music

Traditional Chinese Music, combined with its traditional instruments, is a marvel and one of the greatest aspects of Chinese Culture, old or new.

Modern Chinese Music

The Modern Music of China may not strike you to be any different at all from Western Music. With the generic drum set, electric guitars, headsets and microphones, outdoor stage, and a huge crowd of fans screaming as loud as they can, the setting of a Chinese concert today will bring reminders of the influence of Western Culture on the Chinese society.

再看看西方文化对中国文化的影响吧。不单单是在Music方面，在其他方面的影响也可以这么论述，例如movie industry，traditional customs等方面。

The Sounds of China and the Influence of the West

It's difficult not to spot westernization in major cities of China. As a matter of fact you can find the influence of the Western world in almost every aspect of culture, especially when it comes to entertainment.

Yet today, Chinese pop music dominates the playlist on most Chinese iPods. Whether this is due to the popularity of KTV is up to the individual to decide. When discussing pop music in China, many people talk about musicians from Taiwan, but what makes Taiwan so special when it comes to music? Is it that they are just born good singers or do they have better structures to support aspiring talents in Taiwan?

Miss Qin is a music producer and a singer in Beijing. She explains, "In the music business in Taiwan they learn from Westerners many years earlier than mainlanders. So their music industry is developing better than it is on the mainland. In my childhood most of the music I heard was from Taiwan. Now many Taiwan music companies cultivate emerging singers from the mainland. The mainland singers can develop their careers in Taiwan. It's healthy competition."

In this case, the westernization, which can be found in the music business, means technical and economical progress. But also the sound of the music itself is influenced by many different music styles and artists from Western countries like the UK or the USA. Many Chinese people listen to foreign music and learn from it.

"If you ask me who influenced my music the most, will you laugh at me when I say Michael Jackson? No doubt his sound allowed me to realize the charm of rhythm."

Miss Qin, whose artist name is Nini, originally came from Liaoning Province and started to produce music in 2006. Her aim is to combine traditional Chinese sounds and melodies with rhythms usually found in Western music.

"I like all styles of music, but R&B is my favorite. As a young Chinese woman born in the 1980s, I hope to mix the Chinese elements to it. I always try to find a way to mix the Chinese and foreign styles; what's more, it is accepted by ordinary people."

Chinese pop music was first influenced by Buck Clayton who was credited with bringing American Jazz to China. His music gained popularity in nightclubs and dancehalls across major cities in the 1920s. The influence of Western music gave more opportunities to musicians to express their feelings and ideas in many new and different styles.

Music could be seen as an international language. It connects people and countries and it reflects the positive and negative aspects of our society.

"In my opinion, music is the reaction of our lives and it is spiritual food. Besides I hope people will find the vitality of the Chinese young guys. Their ideas are open and they dare to think without losing the traditional spirit."

● What is the music like in the shopping mall and in the supermarket?

It's usually very light and cheerful, because they want to keep people in a happy mood and keep them buying. I usually don't pay attention to it, but I do think it affects us in a very subtle way, so subtle that we don't even know we are influenced by it when we spill out more money on unnecessary things.

Art and museum / art gallery

● **Do Chinese people appreciate art?**

Actually, it's hard to say because different people may have different answers to this question. But as for me, I think art is very important in my life. It could enhance my living quality. In my leisure time, I would like to play the piano or go to the gallery to enjoy my life. Appreciating art obviously is a good way for me to relax.

● **Why do you think some people spend a fortune on artworks and put it at home?**

The reason is simple! Because they are keen on art and like those artworks very much. Besides, sometimes, the artwork is very precious and it is hard to gain it. So those who know how to appreciate it would like to spend a lot of money on collecting it. Like my grandfather, he spends lots of money on collecting the Chinese traditional paintings. When he looks at those collections, he always has a sense of satisfaction.

● **Where do you usually go for enjoying art?**

If I have a good chance and enough time, I would like to go to the gallery to appreciate some interesting paintings, including the Chinese traditional paintings and foreign oil paintings. I am keen on all kinds of colorful things. I think this is a good method for me to have an eye for beauty and enjoy my life.

● **Are there any art galleries in your hometown?**

Yes, there are many art galleries in my hometown, although most of them are small-scaled. I also would like to go there in my leisure time. They have different kinds of artworks, such as paintings and sculptures. All of them are quite interesting and I like to appreciate them.

● **Is it important for people to go to the art gallery?**

In my opinion, it's significant for us to go to the art gallery. Most experts point out that going to the art gallery is an effective way to ease people's tension from daily life and relax our mind. And I totally agree with that. When I go to the art gallery, I have a sense of satisfactory. Besides, going to the art gallery also could cultivate our sense of beauty. So I think art galleries are important for human beings.

- **What are the different attitudes towards art between young and old?**

Actually, I've never thought about that. Well, let me see, for young people, maybe pursuing art is kind of fashion. Most of them think that it is a symbol of modern lifestyle. However, for the elderly, maybe they don't think that art is necessary for them. Most of the time, art is just a kind of entertainment.

- **What different artworks do the young and the elderly like?**

Well, this question is tough for me. Let me see, young people prefer some modern art, such as some sculptures which have weird design. In contrast, the elderly would like some traditional art. Like my grandfather, he likes Chinese traditional paintings, including beautiful flowers, birds, bamboos and mountains.

- **What type of Chinese traditional arts is popular?**

It's hard to say, but I guess maybe the Chinese traditional painting is the most popular in our country. You know, this kind of art is our cultural heritage that has thousands of years' of history. Most

Chinese people, especially the older generation would like to appreciate this painting to kill time when their old age is boring. Like my grandparents, they like collecting different kinds of traditional paintings, which spices up their life a lot.

- **Do you think the advertisement is a form of arts?**

Absolutely, you know, nowadays, almost every advertment uses many colorful pictures and interesting music to attract the consumers. Before they publicize the advertisement, the director would think about the ideas, the main color and the music. All of these aspects are elements of art. So I think advertisement's are a form of arts.

- **What are the differences between well-made objects and art?**

Well, let me see. In my opinion, well-made objects are more focusing on good quality and being delicate. By contrast, art is special and unique. To some extent, well-made objects are easier to accept by the public than art because the evaluation of art depends on different kinds of people who know how to appreciate art.

- **What are the differences between the Chinese artworks and western ones?**

To be honest, I've never thought about it. Let me see... Generally speaking, the western artworks are more colorful than Chinese ones. Take paintings as an example, most canvas from foreign countries are colorful while our traditional paintings have simple colors such as black or red. Besides, Chinese artworks are more focused on scenery, plants and animals while the theme of those western ones is mostly about religion. So I think these two are the principal differences between Chinese artworks and western ones.

✓Joedy 点评:

对于对比类题目，大家一定要找好标准，不要乱比啊。不然的话，会越比越乱，不单自己搞混了，也把考官搞糊涂了。对比的时候，大家宜由泛到具体。就像上面的对比一样，考生可以先给出 direct response — Generally speaking, the western artworks are more colorful than Chinese ones. 然后展开论证 — Take paintings as an example. 最后总结陈词 — So I think these two are the principal differences between Chinese artworks and western ones. 这样的论证才是清晰的有逻辑的。

- **Do teenagers like foreign artworks?**

Actually, it's hard to say because different teenagers may have different preference about foreign artworks. But I guess maybe they like it. Like my niece, she likes the Barbie doll very much. She always says that her Barbie doll is extremely beautiful and Barbie is the best artwork from foreign country. So I think they might like it.

- **Do you think artists are being well paid nowadays?**

Absolutely, it is believed that artists earn a great deal of money in their life compared with ordinary people. This is the main reason why so many people want to be an artist. When the artists get well-known by playing in a successful movie, especially in the Hollywood movie, they can gain a lot of money and become rich.

- **What should the government do to protect the art?**

There are many methods for the city authorities to protect the art, which is one of the most important things in the society. First of all, the government should issue some effective laws and policies to preserve the art, such as punishing people who destroy the public sculptures as well as stealing the precious paintings from museum. Besides, the government has responsibility

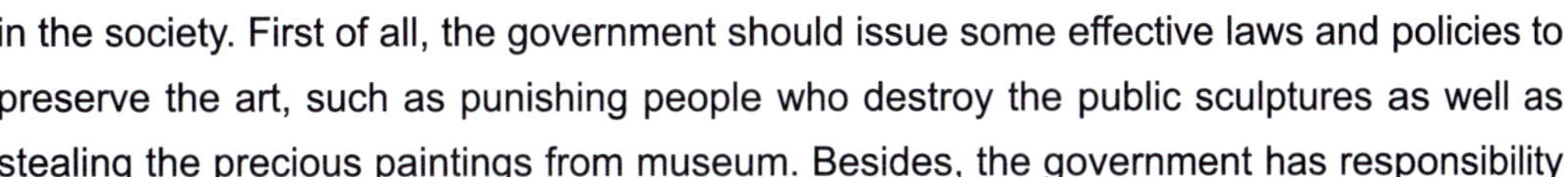

147

to encourage citizens' enthusiasm of art that could enhance people's living standard. Reducing the ticket price of art museum is a good way to achieve the target.

- **Should the government invest more money on art?**

Yes, I think so. In my point of view, art is one of the most important parts for human beings, which could help people enjoy their life more. Without art, our life will become boring and dull. So I think the government has obligation to allocate money on art. The government should build up some art museums and encourage people to appreciate it. Besides, some programs about art such as art learning should be set up by the city authorities. Both of them could help.

Reading

- **What kinds of books are popular among children now?**

I think most of them like to read comic books, especially the Japanese ones, the older kids like to read fantasy books or romantic novels. They mainly like exciting stories.

- **What kinds of books are suitable for children?**

I guess it is books that promote love and peace. Children should not be encouraged to read violent materials. Fairytales and fables are good for them, they teach kids the right ethics and moral, but it seems they are getting less popular nowadays.

- **Is reading important for children?**

Yes, reading helps them develop comprehension ability and helps widen their horizon, they can learn a lot of things from books.

- **Which is better, books or TV?**

Both are good if the correct ones are chosen. Things in books are more in depth and things on TV are more vivid. Documentaries on TV are very educating.

- **Do children in China like reading?**

No, I don't think so. Too much of their attention has been diverted to TV and computer games, they think those are more exciting. And I think schools are not encouraging them to read anything but text books.

● Will e-books replace traditional books in the future?

I don't think so. I think people like real books, the feeling of holding real paper, turning the pages, maybe even the smell of a book; this can never be replaced by e-books. Reading a book on the computer is not very convenient and it tires your eyes out. Even with new, sophisticated viewing devices, I don't believe a real book will ever disappear.

● What should parents do in order to arouse children's interest in reading?

I think it can help a lot when parents take the time to read books to their children when they are young. They will start to really enjoy stories and therefore are more likely to pick up a book themselves when they grow older. Also, when children see their parents read books, they will be more likely to copy that kind of behavior.

✓Joedy 点评：

这是一道典型的"解决类"的问题，考生在简单提出总体解决方案之后，记得要具体把解决方案再进一步论述，要让考官看到考生解决问题的诚意。来看看西方家长如何鼓励孩子读书的吧。

15 Ways for Parents to Encourage Reading

The following are some ways to turn a young reader's reluctance into enthusiasm:

1. Interest is the best teacher. Parents are advised to use children's interest and hobbies as starting point, and scout for things your kids might like to read. Parents should also be able to notice what attract kids' attention, and then build on that interest.

2. Create an atmospheric surrounding of reading at home by leaving all types of books, magazines and colorful catalogs in conspicuous places. Set aside a special place for children to keep their own books. It can also be achieved when parents let children see them reading for pleasure at home or deliberately show unwillingness to drop reading for other activities.

3. Make it a rule for the whole family to spend some time reading on a regular basis, and this can be achieved in many ways, not just at home. You can either do it by taking your children to the library or bookshops where a children's section can be found. Explore the children's section together.

4. Relate reading to other activities: a way to gather useful information for, say, making paper airplanes, or organizing a family trip. Design games that are reading-related, like spelling games and board games in which players are required to read cards and directions.

5. Encourage older children to read to their younger brothers and sisters. Older children enjoy showing off their skills to an admiring audience.

6. Share your reactions to things you read with your child in a casual and friend-like way, and encourage your children to do likewise.

7. Read aloud to your child, especially a child who is discouraged by his or her own poor reading skills. The pleasure of listening to your reading, rather than struggling alone, may restore your child's initial enthusiasm for books and reading.

8. Encourage your child to read aloud to you an exciting passage in a book, or a joke in a joke book. When children read aloud, do remember not to point out every single mistake they make because you would put them off by doing so.

9. Give books and magazines based on your child's current interests on gift-giving occasions. Of course do not overdo it for the obvious reason that it may bore your children.

10. Introduce the bookmark. Remind your youngster that you don't have to finish a book in one sitting; you can stop after a few pages, or a chapter, and pick up where you left off at another time. Don't try to persuade your child to finish a book he or she doesn't like. Recommend putting the book aside and trying another.

11. Treat your children to an evening of laughter and entertainment featuring books! Many children (parents, too) regard reading as a serious activity. Sharing a joke in a joke book or a funny tidbit in newspapers can spice up the reading activity.

12. Extend your child's positive reading experiences. For example, if your youngster enjoys a book about dinosaurs, follow up with a visit to a natural history museum.

13. Offer other special incentives to encourage your child's reading. Allow your youngster to stay up an extra 15 minutes to finish a chapter; promise to take your child to see a movie after he or she has finished the book on which it was based; relieve your child of a regular chore to free up time for reading.

14. Limit your children's TV viewing in an effort to make time for other activities, such as reading. But never use TV as a reward for reading, or a punishment for not reading.

15. Create opportunities for children to read, as not all the reading takes place in books. For example, while dining out, encourage children to read the menus and food labels. These spur-of-the-moment opportunities can be greater fun than normal reading.

✓Joedy 提醒：

看到了吗？方法是每个人都不一样的，而且每个方法都不一定是尽善尽美的，大家在提出解决方案的时候不要去刻意追求方案的完全可行性和完美度。最重要的是展示给考官，考生解决问题的诚意就好，所以以上所提供给大家的方案，大家只需选择其中一到两种展开论述就好。

● Are teachers playing a more important role in guiding children?

Sadly enough, teachers are more and more taking on the role of parents. Parents often don't have the time to raise their own children and often let grandparents take care of their children. If a child does not receive a decent upbringing, they will become difficult to handle, egotistical and self-centered. I don't believe it is the job of a teacher to replace parents, but sometimes it seems that parents do not take their role seriously and teachers are forced to step in.

● How is the Internet used in libraries?

People in libraries use computers with an Internet connection for the same purpose as at home, to look up information, to download music, to view movies or maybe even to play games.

● How can more people be attracted to libraries?

By providing secondary services like a café where you can drink a nice cup of coffee, or by providing free computers with Internet access. Also a library can organize courses or other interesting activities to attract more visitors.

● How will libraries in the future be like?

I think in the future libraries will have become a multi-functional unit within urban society where citizens can meet and exchange ideas. A library can become a platform for different groups in society where people can intermingle and where bridges between different cultures, education levels and social positions can be built.

✓Joedy 点评:

这是一道"展望类"的题型，对于展望型的题目，如之前说的，大家要大胆预测。毕竟 with the development of modern technology，大家现在的确可以大胆对将来进行展望啊!

The Library of the Future

Forecasting changes in the future is, in most cases, an enterprise of questioning. This essay is devoted to imaginations concerning the possible future of a system providing information via books, which is once called libraries. When looking toward the future, there are many questions. What are we going to find when we visit a library / media center in the future? Will we have robots as librarians rather than human beings in libraries? Will there be even more feet of shelving to house books? Will there still be books, as we know them today?

The traditional library, widely used and considered as a place for book storage and students to study, will become out-of-date. It has been a time-consuming daily routine for students to "commute" from general classrooms to a library for resource materials, and then to the computer lab to complete an assignment. Traditionally, school libraries have been vulnerable to budget cuts, and the irreversible trend of school moving technology into classroom is going to worsen the situation.

The traditional form of school library, built of bricks and mortar, is being converted into the one constructed with bits and bytes. This means that the library of the future possibly may not have four walls and racks of tangible books.

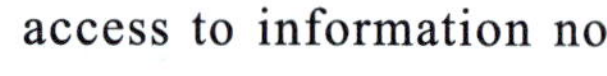

The worst-case scenario is that new technology and electronic access to information not only threatens to eliminate school libraries but also those who have been serving as information-tellers. Teachers specializing in such fields as art, music, physical education and library / media, are losing positions in order to carve up the needed dollars for reduced class size and the purchase of new technologies.

Looking into the future nationwide, advanced

technologies such as on-line catalogs, district wide networks, and presentation software are being introduced to school libraries. There is so much content out there that it is impossible to keep urging school administrators to focus on process, on the ability to find and use information for a purpose. In view of a disconcerting fact that students of today have been overloaded with information from various sources, libraries / media centers in the future must be designed to prepare students to make critical judgments about this flood of electronic information.

The library / media center of future is bound to be a place where instructions about how to adapt to the new world of digital information are given. Library / Media center technology will reach beyond school walls by way of the Internet to put information resources into the hands of end-users. Therefore, with networks linking all areas of the modern school, a library in traditional style is too limited for access to information.

Acquisitions and selection criteria will take on an entirely new meaning when considering access to on-line services. The information explosion has created far more information than one school library which could possibly contain within its walls. The information contained on the Internet, the global network of computer networks, is richer than any school which can afford to acquire.

Librarians and media specialists will strike out into classrooms to consult with teachers. There they will suggest resources, locate and acquire needed materials, recommend strategies, facilitate use of technologies, and instruct students and teachers in optimal information-seeking methods. Many traditional tasks will be assigned to clerks, leaving the professional free to work directly with students and teachers. As students become more self-directed learners, the media specialist will act as a resource person to support information and develop appropriate presentation strategies.

While nobody is advocating the abolition of text-based libraries, electronic storage and telecommunications technologies will vastly increase the variety of information available and the number of people who have access to it.

✓Joedy 提醒：

对于将来的展望，大家可以在基于现实不足的基础上大胆地预测，毕竟人类的不断向前发展都是由对现实的不满而推动的。考生在论述时，可以加上对现实状况的描述，这样显得更有根有据啊。

第7节　People and Relationship

Lesson 1 Part 1 听题训练

在relationship这个话题里，雅思口语考试近几年考得最多的关系就是"朋友关系"，"家庭关系"以及"同事关系"，其中前两者考得最频繁。所以我特地选择前两类话题中常见的话题给各位考生。不过问题倒挺常规的，没有特别难的题目。大家好好朗读一下吧。

Friends

- Do you like making friends?
- Do you like hanging out with your friends?
- How often do you go out with your friends?
- What do you usually do with your friends?
- Who do you like making friends with more, the young or the old?
- How do people make friends nowadays?
- Have you ever made any friends on the Internet?
- Is friendship important in your life?
- How do you choose friends?
- Do you like to have one or two close friends or more common friends?
- How do you keep a good relationship with your friends?
- How is your friendship different between now and in you childhood?

<table>
<tr><td>Family</td></tr>
</table>

- How big is your family?

- Do you live together with your parents?

- Do you prefer to live by yourself or live with your parents?

- How much time do you spend with your family and relatives?

- What sorts of things do you like to do together with your family members?

- Would you like to be with your family or your friends? Why?

Lesson2 Part 1 真题点评与参考答案

Friends

● Do you like making friends?

Well, of course. Actually, I suppose that making friends plays an important role in my life, and I have a lot of friends, both close and common ones.

● Do you like hanging out with your friends?

Certainly, in most of the time I'm quite keen on hanging out with friends, because I think that it is a process to know more about my friends. Also it will become a beautiful memory in our life.

● How often do you go out with your friends?

Well, to be honest, I should say that it really depends. For instance, I will go out with my friends three or four times a week during long holidays. But if I'm at school, I will meet them almost twice a week.

● **What do you usually do with your friends?**

I will do shopping with my friends most of the time. The reason is that we can get more suggestions from each other before making decisions. And some of my friends are good at bargaining, too.

● **Who do you like making friends with more, the young or the old?**

Well, virtually I like making friends with both the young and the old because I can get more knowledge from the old and at the same time I will gain fresh ideas and energy from the young.

● **How do people make friends nowadays?**

Well, there are various ways of making friends in the modern world. Generally, for people it's easy to make friends at school or working places. And some are used to making fiends at parties or special meetings.

● **Have you ever made any friends on the Internet?**

Well, sometimes I think I'm a traditional girl so I do not choose this way to make friends. I consider the relationship on the Internet not as real or strong as to share my feelings with someone I don't know.

● **Is friendship important in your life?**

Well, friendship is an essential part in my life just like the air. I will share with my friends something that I don't usually talk about with my parents. They are truly important for me and become another kind of family.

● **How do you choose friends?**

In my opinion, I prefer to choose friends by the feelings other than their status of society. The reason would be that a friend is a person for me who can share pressure or tell me the solution rather than helping me in a material way.

✓**Joedy 点评**:

How类型的问题有时是问"程度"的，例如：How important are friends to you? 有时又是问"方式"的，例如本题：How do you choose a friend?

大家在听题目的时候一定要留意，不要听错重点啊！

看看下面的背景资料：

1. http://www.ehow.com

How to Choose Friends

There is nothing better than being surrounded by good friends. You may look at some people and their friends with envy as they chat away happily and participate in activities together. It may be hard to figure out where to start in your search for good friends. There are many things to keep in mind when choosing people to consider as friends.

Step 1

Find people with similar interests as you. Join a group or class that meets for activities such as biking, bird watching, scrap-booking or aerobics.

Step 2

Do not disclose too much personal information immediately. Trust is a big part of working relationships. Make sure that the people you are considering as friends are people you want to be known more intimate details of your life.

Step 3

Choose a friend that gives and takes in the relationship as much as you do. Friendship is a two-way street, one person cannot make a relationship work.

Step 4

Look for personalities that compliment you own. Groups of friends have similar interests but also have qualities that make up for traits that others in the group do not have.

Step 5

Choose friends that make you feel that you are best. It is important to surround yourself with positive people who genuinely want you to continue to be better and happier in your life.

Step 6

Be picky. Just because someone is nice and has similar interests as you do does not mean you have to be their friend. Friendship takes time and effort, it is an investment.

Step 7

Invest wisely. Make sure that you do not waste your energies on half-hearted or fair-weather friends. The friends you choose can enrich your life or take you on a negative roller-coaster of time and feelings.

2. http://www.wikihow.com

How to choose a friend

Some people have known their best friends for years, and eventually question themselves: Did I make the right decision? Is my friend still my friend? Are we growing apart? Here's an article which will help you to smooth out these worries.

Please read on…

1. Start a conversation with your friend. If they immediately launch into it enthusiastically, they're a friend. If they make a joke out of it, start to brag about themselves, say (for example) "shut up, Lawler", or simply ignore you, they're in a bad mood or they are not a friend.

2. If you're still not sure: act excited about something that you're doing. If they simply grunt and show no interest or start talking about themselves they're self-centered and definitely not your friend.

3. Look out for signs: If you see your friend talking about you behind your back, calling you weird, care only about themselves and tease you... I don't need to say anymore.

4. Dump your so-called friend and move on. Talk to other people. A real friend is one who listens, who is honest and true, and as kind as they can be. Nuff said.

● Do you like to have one or two close friends or more common friends?

Well, according to a Chinese proverb, "It is really enough to have a bosom friend in life", I suppose that having one or two close friends is more important and more beneficial for people.

● How do you keep a good relationship with your friends?

Right, I believe that keeping a good relationship is not only my business but also my friends'. However, I usually get in touch with my friends by e-mail or telephone when there is a long distance between us.

● How is your friendship different between now and in your childhood?

Well, I would like to say that the friendship in my childhood was simple. Children like to play together just for fun, and most of my friends in that period were at the same age. By contrast, the friendship now is more complicated. We can get to know many different people, and know much about things of society.

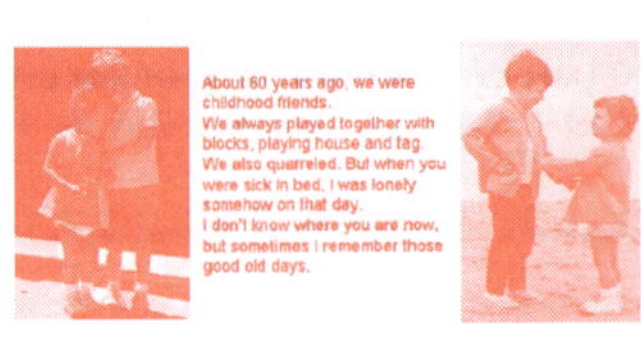

Family

● How big is your family?

My family is a nuclear family including my father，mother and me.

● Do you live together with your parents?

Yes, we live in a small apartment in Guangzhou.

● Do you prefer to live by yourself or live with your parents?

Well, I would like to live by myself when I am a student, because I can learn more things and become more independent. However, when my parents become old, I prefer to stay with them and take care of them. It is after all my obligation as a daughter.

● How much time do you spend with your family and relatives?

Well, you know, I should continue my study, so the time I spend with my family is not so much, maybe only on weekends. However, all of us cherish the time when we are together.

● What sorts of things do you like to do together with your family members?

As for me, I would like to have a walk in a park or go to an art gallery with my family. It is not only a good way to unwind but also a kind of communication between me and my family.

● Would you like to be with your family or your friends? Why?

Well, virtually I prefer to be with my friends but it does not mean that I don't love my family. I feel that parents always regard their children as babies, and most of time they think they are right and they won't listen to us. Whereas, it is more free to stay with friends since they would like to listen to your feelings or opinions.

Lesson 3 Part 2 审题训练与真题讲解

★ Cue card 1 审题训练

> Describe a family member who you spend most time with.
>
> You should say:
>
> Who he / she is.
>
> What his / her relationship with you is.
>
> What personality he / she has.
>
> What you do together.
>
> And explain the reason why you like spending most time with him / her.

✓Joedy 提醒：

A family member 是近来最有代表性的一张"人物类"的卡片，其转题的灵活性很高，例如可以转成 your best friend（妈妈可以是自己的好朋友啊），也可以是 a person who is good at his / her job（妈妈是位成功的妈妈），又或者是 an elderly person you admire（如果妈妈不够老，把描述妈妈的语言转成讲奶奶），还可以是 a person who is good at cooking（当然是妈妈啦），当然更可以是 a teacher you like the best（父母是我们的第一个老师）。其实所有被考生选到的人物都是对自己产生过影响的，不然为什么要选择他/她呢。好了，现在大家来想想讲什么比较好。

★ Cue card 1真题点评与参考答案

The person I would like to spend most of time with is my mother. My mother is a kind and gentle woman. She is very busy from morning till night. As a teacher she works diligently and efficiently. As a mother, she takes good care of us and gives us every comfort. I have an elder brother. He and I both love her dearly, as she loves us.

My mother has been teaching maths at a middle school in my home town. She goes to the school early in the morning and does not return home until late in the afternoon. She loves her students and cares for them. She treats them with patience and teaches them well. For her excellent qualities and good teaching results, she is always praised and respected by both her students and colleagues alike. And she has been chosen or elected as a model teacher several times. I am so proud of her.

The most amazing thing is that while working so hard, my mom can still take good care of me and always show her love and concern to me. When she is not working, we cook together and we talk, and it is always a pleasant thing to talk to her about her students. My mother is great indeed, and that's why I like spending time with her.

✓Joedy 点评：

Part 2经常会考关于各种人物的描述，包括老人、朋友、小孩……这时候大家就需要掌握一些常见的具有代表性的思路以及表达方式了。

描述人的时候，通常可以包括以下思路：

1. What's the relationship between you and the person? / How did you get to know the person?

2. What kind of person he / she is?

3. What influence does this person have on you? / Why do you like this person?

凡是讲到人物类的话题，建议大家多点从"此人对自己产生的影响"这方面扩展，这样才能说出真情实感来，否则就会显得很dry，流水账式的描述是没有人愿意听的。例如讲到family member这一话题，可以选择突出"亲情"这个概念，凸显家庭成员对自己的成长带来的影响，这个影响可以包括很多方面啊，例如：well-mannered有礼貌的，compassionate有爱心的，confident自信的，industrious勤奋的，optimistic乐观的，level-headed遇事冷静的，modest谦虚的，considerate体贴的，versatile多才多艺的。

当然，单纯堆砌一堆形容词，是没办法说服人的。所以，大家要在一个点上重点扩展说，例如想要充分表现此人的considerate，就要拿出"真凭实据"——实例，让此人的待人体贴的一面得到充分的展示。也就是说，大家平时生活要多点养成叙事的习惯，不要仅仅是摆弄一两个词汇。

★ Cue card 2审题训练

> Describe a famous person / a celebrity you want to meet.
>
> You should say:
>
> Who he / she is.
>
> What kind of person he / she is.
>
> When you first saw / heard about him / her.
>
> What you plan to do for meeting him.
>
> And explain the reason why you want to meet him / her.

✓Joedy 提醒：

　　A famous person也是考得频率很高的一张卡片，一般考生想到famous person都会想到一些伟人，然后用很大的篇幅去描述此名人的丰功伟绩。其实这样往往是吃力不讨好的，很多时候考官都误认为考生从哪个网站上抄来一篇名人简介，这样无论讲得多好，分数都不会很如意的。其实famous person除了走常规路线讲一些明星或者伟人外，还有一些社会名人（例如"感动中国年度人物"），这些人的事迹容易和大家的生活联系起来，更容易打动考官。大家想想，讲谁比较好呢？

★ Cue card 2真题点评与参考答案

Well, the person I am going to talk about is Jet Li, who is one of the most famous kungfu and action movie stars both at home and abroad. Actually, as a girl, I am not quite keen on that kind of films. However, I know about and admire Jet Li not from his movies but his One Foundation Project.

There was a great loss in Sichuan by severe earthquakes on May 12, and millions of people lost their homes and family. When Jet Li knew that, who was one of the lucky survivors in Indian Ocean Tsunami, he thought about a lot of what he can do for the victims, because he knew what was the true feeling when people faced death and how important to show love to them. So he set up One Foundation which means it is a sustainable, professional, and trustworthy foundation.

If I had the chance to meet him, I would give him my donation which I deposit every month, and sincerely tell him that his project is meaningful not only for the victims but for everyone who lives in the world as well. I guess he will be happy to see what I do.

✓Joedy 点评：

这篇对于李连杰的描述非常精彩，优点有二：

1. 很好地运用了我在上课时讲过的"抓大放小"原则——抓住自己擅长的熟悉的方面扩展，对于不熟悉的方面快速带过。该考生并没有在李连杰的演艺成就上作过多描述，而是集中精力讲了李连杰在慈善方面的成就。这样很好地做到了扬长避短。

2. 联系自己的感受，讲述真实情感——该考生并没有如旁观者一样去描述李连杰，而是把李连杰的成就与自己的感受联系在一起，显得非常自然不做作容易打动考官，又避开了背答案的嫌疑，一举两得。

Lesson 4 Part 3 听题训练

✓Joedy 提醒：

讲到relationship，到了Part 3的问题涉及的面会更广更深了。例如，考生会被问到generation gap的问题，也会被问到one-child policy的问题，另外还有responsibility的方面。大家做好准备了吗？是否有足够的信心一下子就能反应过来考官在问什么呢？

Family and friends

- How often do your family members get together?

- What do you usually do with your family members when going out?

- Is it necessary to spend much time with the family members?

- How many generations will usually live together in China?

- What do you think of the one-child policy in China?

- What are the upsides and downsides of a child living with parents?

- What are the advantages and disadvantages of living with a big family?

- What are the advantages of good family relationship?

- What's different between man and woman's role in a family?

- Who should shoulder the responsibility of taking care of the child in the family, father or mother?

- Is there a generation gap between the old and the young now?

- What responsibilities should children take for parents?

- How do Chinese people take care of the elderly?

- What is the difference between the help you get from family and from your friends?

Famous people

- Do you want to become famous?

- Why do people like to become famous?

- What are the advantages and disadvantages of becoming famous?

- Does every famous person make great contribution to the society?

- What do you think of getting famous through the Internet?

Lesson 5 Part 3 真题讲解与参考答案

Family and friends

● How often do your family members get together?

All of us are living at home, so we can share time together every night. After school or after work, we can have dinner together. We can also enjoy a movie after that.

● What do you usually do with your family members when going out?

When we go out, we usually have meals with their friends or some relatives. My parents love to communicate with others, and we also like tasting the delicious food.

● Is it necessary to spend much time with the family members?

I think so. In my opinion, family is the most important thing. We should cherish our family members. The work puts lots of pressure on us, and the leisure time with family can make us relaxed and unwind.

● How many generations will usually live together in China?

I think most of Chinese families now are nuclear families. When the children started their work, they would leave their parents and rent houses for more convenience to work. When they set up new families, they will buy houses, then to live with their children.

● What do you think of the one-child policy in China?

I think it's reasonable. China has the greatest number of population in the world. There is less and less space to live in, and the resources are also not plenty enough for so many people. So the one-child policy helps to solve such problems.

● What are the upsides and downsides of a child living with parents?

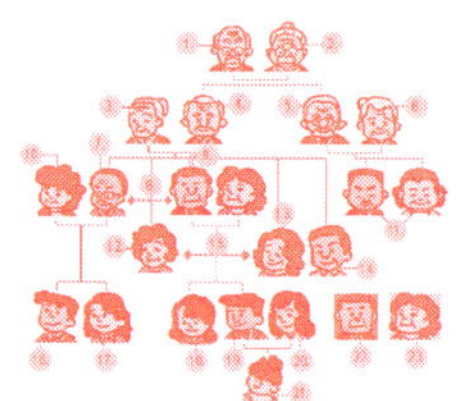

The upsides for children is that they can be protected by parents, and have more time to communicate with each other. On the other hand, they are dependent on parents, since they are used to counting on parents and have less courage to face the difficulties.

● What are the advantages and disadvantages of living with a big family?

Living with a big family provides a lot of fun to people, since there are many family members around, like singing karaoke or traveling. But the disadvantages are also significant. The problem of privacy is a headache. People will not have so much private space to stay alone.

● What are the advantages of good family relationship?

Good family relationships can help me relax in my life. And it also gives me lots of encouragement, making me feel strong with a lot of wonderful support. I am always proud that I have a close relationship with my parents, which helped me to grow up into an outgoing and open-minded person.

● What's different between man and woman's role in a family?

I think there is not so much difference nowadays. A woman is not only a housewife, but also bear the same financial pressure as a man. And most of men today will share with the housework after work.

● Who should shoulder the responsibility of taking care of the child in the family, father or mother?

Both of them should shoulder the responsibility, because they are both parents of the child. Children need care from both father and mother. Take my family as a good example, when I stay with my father, I feel the strong sense of security for I always know that he will protect me, and with mother, I can get more delicate care. Mother will take care of all the chores which can make life easier.

- Is there a generation gap between the old and the young now?

I think so. The problem of communication has always existed from the past to the future. The young would like to talk more about risk and adventure, for example, while the old prefer the practical living style.

- What responsibilities should children take for parents?

I think children should respect their parents and take care of them when they are getting old. For example, most children nowadays will take their parents to travel every year and enjoy great time together.

- How do Chinese people take care of the elderly?

Most young people prefer to hire someone to take care of the elderly, because the young are too busy to handle all the daily things. Many of us have a housekeeper to help us cope with the daily household chores at home.

- What is the difference between the help you get from family and from your friends?

I think family members will be more helpful with the bigger issues like finding a job for me, or giving me some financial help. Friends are not as close as family. I will not receive the financial help from friends. In my experience, friends also gave me a hand in the daily issues like helping me return the books to the library or borrowing something.

Famous people

- Do you want to become famous?

Well, I don't think so. I just want to be this person who can do what I like, and I can help the people around me by this process. Being famous is stressful to me since everyone surrounding will pay lots of attention to my daily life.

- Why do people like to become famous?

Right, I suppose that there are many different reasons for people wanting to become famous. Some pursue the money, and some seek fame. However, in my opinion, most people just want to make their dream come true, and only these people can become great men.

- What are the advantages and disadvantages of becoming famous?

Proverb always says that one gets something while loses something. When one becomes famous, he will get more attention from other people, and he has great influence on the society. However, he may spend less time with his friends or family, and he can not go to the public places easily.

● Does every famous person make great contribution to the society?

Definitely not. For me, a famous person does not mean he is kind or willing to help others. Maybe he just gains great success in his field. Of course, we are happy to see that more and more famous people realize that they should make more contribution to the society because they have to be good models in society.

● What do you think of getting famous through the Internet?

Right, the Internet plays a more and more essential role in our life, and we find it a shortcut to be famous. Many people can get famous overnight through the Internet.

✓ Joedy 点评：

雅思口语考试是绝对跟得上形势的，探讨的话题都是现在社会很热门的话题，毕竟考官也是生活在我们社会的一分子嘛。像名人的影响啊，如何成名啊这些话题，考官也很想知道我们的国家与他们的国家是否一样呢！

来看看一个wikiHow对于如何成名作出的精辟讲解，很独到。

How to Become Famous

One can get famous in many different ways and the important step is for you to become outstanding in whatever area you choose. There are famous cooks, artists, chefs, athletes. But no matter what field or interest you select, you will require training, experience and most of all — persistence.

Understand that there is not one path to fame. There are practically as many paths to fame as there are famous people. That said, here are four generic techniques that would apply in many situations:

1. Be the best at something and the first to do something. Research and find something that no one has ever done, and do it. Look around and see what someone famous is famous for, and learn to do it better. Be a better runner, or seamstress, singer or dancer or an outstanding mother or father. Select a particular interest and become the best at it.

2. Try to be the worst at something. Tiny Tim became famous for singing in a falsetto voice. He was really bad. That made him different and famous. William Hung did the same thing more recently on American Idol. He sings so badly that people flock to see him perform.

3. Being radically different or being overly generous will make people notice, and you in turn will become famous. Notice how some overweight women have recently become models, and are pictured on calendars and starred in hit movies, and become famous almost overnight.

4. Know that just by being in the right place, at the right time, can make you famous, maybe only for an hour, but at that time, everyone will know who you are. Liken yourself to the fireman who pulled the child out of the well. We do not remember his name now, but at the time of the happening, everyone knew him, he was televised, and became instantly and briefly famous.

Use a famous platform like http://myspace.com, http://youtube.com, http://www.gotcast.com, to showcase your skills.

Whether you're a singer, actor, or have other talents, it helps to get noticed for what you do and using video on the above websites will help. There have been many people that have used websites such as Myspace to present their skills and earn themselves famous recognition. Just make sure you really want to be famous first...

Remember, don't follow your dreams — chase them.

第 *8* 节　Event and Experience

Lesson 1 Part 1 听题训练

好了，来到了最后一个章节，我们要谈论"经历"了。其实人们的生活就是由无数的经历组成的，经历里会有"人物"，会有"地点"，会有涉及的"物品"，也有其主要的"故事"情节，经历里有"成功"的喜悦，也有在困难时的"成长与变化"。可以说，这一节是之前所有话题的集合。大家要好好朗读一下了。体会一下一般会问到什么问题吧。

Party
● Do you like attending parties? When do people have parties?
● Do Chinese people like parties? Why do some people hate going there?
● What do you dislike at the party?
● Do you like attending family parties or friend gatherings? Why?
● Do the young or the old like going to the party? Why?

<table>
<tr><td align="center">Visit</td></tr>
<tr><td>

● How often do you have guests at home?

● What preparations do you make when someone visits you at home?

● Do you like to have others visit at home?

</td></tr>
</table>

<table>
<tr><td align="center">Birthday</td></tr>
<tr><td>

● How did you celebrate your last birthday?

● How do people celebrate birthdays in your country?

● How do children and the elderly celebrate their birthday respectively?

● Do you think birthday is a special day for people?

● People say birthdays are more special and important for children than adults, what do you think?

● How important is birthday to children?

</td></tr>
</table>

Party

● Do you like attending parties? When do people have parties?

Yes, I like to attend parties if I have enough time and chance, I think this is a good way for me to relax and communicate with my friends. I think people prefer to hold parties on their birthday or some other important occasions such as graduation ceremony and a wedding. All of these kinds of beautiful moments are worth celebrating.

✓Joedy 点评：

人们在不同的日子会有不同的party，我来给大家总结一下到底有哪些是在西方非常常见的，大家可以对比一下与我们国家的有什么不同。

at-home party 家庭宴会	surprise party 惊喜派对
tea party 茶会	welcome meeting 欢迎会
luncheon party 午餐会	farewell party 惜别会
dinner party 晚餐会	house-warming party 暖屋会
garden party 游园会	wedding reception 结婚宴会
cocktail party 鸡尾酒会	birthday party 生日宴会
picnic party 野餐会	fancy ball 化装舞会
potluck party 家常聚餐会	banquet 酒宴
graduation party 毕业聚会	

● Do Chinese people like parties? Why do some people hate going there?

Yes, I think so, especially the younger generation likes to have parties. Because they are young and energetic, and joining parties can help them to ease the tension from daily life. Actually, I have no idea about why some people don't like to go there. I guess maybe they think the parties are too noisy sometimes and making them feel uncomfortable.

● What do you dislike at the party?

Well, it is hard to say because I like the party. Um! If I have to say something I dislike at the party, I think maybe the noise. Sometimes the noises are very loud at the parties and make me feel annoyed and uncomfortable.

● Do you like attending family parties or friend gatherings? Why?

Generally speaking, I prefer friend gatherings because I feel free when I get along with my friends. We can talk about everything we want and do everything we like. Whereas attending family parties, most of times are very formal and I must dress formally, which makes me feel a little uncomfortable. So I like friend gatherings more than attending family parties.

● Do the young or the old like going to the party? Why?

Well, in my opinion, I think the younger generation likes going to the party more because they are young and energetic. Most of them like my friends prefer to go to the parties to relax and relieve the pressure from work, study and relationship. Whereas the old think that parties have too much noise so they don't like them. It makes them feel annoyed and uncomfortable. And my parents always say that parties are the young people's thing. So I think young people like going to the party more than the old.

Visit

● How often do you have guests at home?

Actually, it is not too often, just about once a month. My parents are very busy with their business and I live on the campus. Only sometimes at the weekend, when my parents have time to stay at home and I can go back home, can we invite some relatives or friends to my home. But it is not too often.

● **What preparations do you make when someone visits you at home?**

Well, let me see. If someone is going to visit my home, I will clean my home before he / she comes at first. I want to make them feel like home. I also will prepare some snacks on the tea table, such as candies and nuts. And I will try my best to give them a warm welcome and make them feel comfortable.

● **Do you like to have others visit at home?**

Well, it depends. If I am in my leisure time, I would like to give the warm welcome to my friends when they visit my home and I think they will have a good time with me. But if someone visits me uninvited when I am busy with my own business, it may give me a headache and I'll feel annoyed.

Birthday

● **How did you celebrate your last birthday?**

Last birthday, I hung out with my friends. We went to watch an interesting movie and we played the electronic games in Tianhe Town. In the evening, we held the birthday party at home with my friends, blowing out the candles and eating the delicious cake. We had fun at that night.

● **How do people celebrate birthdays in your country?**

Well, it is hard to say because different people may have different preference. But I think the younger generation in my country prefers to hold a birthday party and invite their good friends to celebrate it, whereas the old people would like to eat out with the whole family. They will gather together and enjoy the big feast. This is also a good chance for them to communicate with each other.

✓Joedy 点评：

看看摘自http://www.chinaculture.org的背景资料。

A Typical Chinese Birthday Bash

In almost every country in the world, birthdays are regarded as great occasions. Some birthday traditions are quite similar in many parts of the world, such as blowing out candles to make a wish and friendly pinches or taps for good luck in the coming year, while other traditions are catered to suit different cultures.

Traditionally, Chinese people don't attach much attention to their birthdays until they reach a certain age. However, they do celebrate birthdays for newborns and elderly people by inviting relatives and close friends to banquets that feature various activities.

Nowadays, young people in China also celebrate their birthdays every year, although the celebrations for newborns and the elderly are still more elaborate. Traditionally, Chinese people do not pay much attention to birthdays until they reach 60 years old of age. The 60th birthday is regarded as an important milestone in life and therefore is often a big celebration. After the 60th birthday, a celebration is held every 10 years. Generally, the older the person is, the more elaborate the celebration.

To make the occasion grander, other relatives and friends are also invited. In Chinese culture, 60 years completes a life cycle and 61 is regarded as the beginning of a new life cycle. When one reaches 60, he or she is expected to have a big family filled with children and grandchildren. It is an age to be proud of.

It is often the adult sons and daughters who celebrate their elderly parents' birthdays to show their respect and express thanks. According to traditional custom, parents are offered foods with auspicious connotations. On the morning of his or her birthday, the father or mother eats a bowl of "long-life noodles". In China, long noodles symbolizes longevity. Eggs are also among the best choices of foods eaten on this special occasion.

Regardless of the scale of the celebration, "peaches" (which are not really peaches but steamed wheat shaped like a peach with sweet stuffing) and noodles, which are both signs of long life, are staples. When the noodles are cooked, they should not be cut since short noodles may bring bad luck. Everyone at the feast eats these two types of foods to extend their warm wishes to the star of the show.

Typical birthday presents involve two or four of each of the following: eggs, long noodles, artificial peaches, tonics, wine and money wrapped in red paper.

● How do children and the elderly celebrate their birthday respectively?

As I said before, the younger generation in my country prefers to hold a birthday party and invite their good friends to celebrate it, whereas the old people would like to eat out with the whole family. They celebrate birthdays in two completely different ways.

● Do you think birthday is a special day for people?

Absolutely, I think birthday are very important for every one, either the children or the old. In my opinion, a birthday is a symbol of growing up and getting more mature. It is also a meaningful time in people's life which deserves to be celebrated. So I think a birthday is a special day for people.

✓ Joedy 点评：

对于birthday是否重要，来听听大家怎么说。

Is your birthday important to you? Why?

I didn't use to think my birthday was all that important to me. In the entire time I've been working, I don't think I've ever taken a day off for my birthday specifically, as I understood that even if I took the day off, my husband would have to take a vacation day also to have the time with me. I just celebrate it on the nearest weekend with a few friends — don't expect any presents, just enjoy going out and having a nice meal together, nothing more really than we do at other time during the year, anyway.

However, there was one year at my old workplace when a co-worker who was there briefly shared a birthday with me. Although we were in different departments, it was a small business, and I noticed as everyone made a tremendous fuss over her birthday and no one ever mentioned mine at all. It was kind of hurtful.

So I don't necessarily think it's silly for those who wish to have the days recognized by their friends and loved ones. That year I certainly wished a few people had made a bigger fuss, or my husband had sent flowers to me at work so others would know that it was my birthday, too.

I think birthdays are actually pretty sad from a certain point of life, I see it as a reminder that I'm one year closer to the end... (whenever the end is)

I don't particularly care about my birthday, however being surprised by a loved one just to make me know how much they care is nice. I usually treat it as any other day.

Well for me, I don't expect everyone to stop everything just for me, but as long as I get together with friends / family and celebrate (big or small) then I'm happy.

It's such a built up thing from babies, we know it's a very special day and carry it through our life. It's the one day of the year that is all about you!

As I was younger it mattered more. Nothing changes when you turn a year older — the day of your birthday, you don't feel any different than the day before. It's just a number. When I turned 25 and had a perfect driving record, I remembered that my car insurance would drop. It didn't. That was disappointing, so I guess basically what I am saying is that the perks of birthdays stop after turning 21. Because at 16 you can drive, at 18 you can vote and join the military, and at 21 you are able to legally drink. I don't have anything else to look forward to until I am considered a senior citizen which I have almost 25 years to go for that. I used to look forward to the day I would be able to retire, and would count down by my birthdays, but since social security will probably no longer be

in practice by the time I am old enough to utilize it, it will no longer matter as I will probably have to work until the day I die.

● People say birthdays are more special and important for children than adults, what do you think?

Actually, I don't think so. I think a birthday is equally important for children and adults. A birthday is a symbol of growing up for children and it also means getting more mature and gaining more experience in life for the old. It is the same meaningful for both groups and needs to be celebrated by both young and the old.

● How important is birthday to children?

Well, this question is a tough one for me. Let me see. I believe that almost every child likes birthdays. When I was a child, I really wanted to have a birthday because at the birthday, I could receive many presents from my parents and little friends, such as little dolls or toys. I also could blow out the candles and eat the delicious cakes. It was very fun and happy. So I think all of these are very important for children. It is also a beautiful memory for them when they grow up, like me.

Lesson 3 Part 2 审题训练与真题讲解

★ Cue card 1 审题训练

Describe an interesting story you know from TV / newspaper.

You should say:

    What it is about.

    When you heard about it.

    Who were involved in it.

And explain the reason why this story was interesting to you.

✓Joedy 提醒：

    An interesting story是非常有代表性的一张经典卡片，其转题的灵活性也很高，故事里的"人物"可以讲人物，例如：a movie character you like或者a person you admire；故事里的"地点"就可以讲地方，例如：a place you most want to go in the world；故事里的情节更加可以转成所有故事，例如：a movie you like best或a book you like，又或者是a song you like（讲歌曲背后的故事）。所以大家要好好准备一个故事，想想吧。写下key words。

★ **Cue card 1真题点评与参考答案**

I would like to share with you the story of DORAEMON (多啦A梦), the most famous cartoon character in all of Japan .

It is a humorous children's story about a boy named Nobita（大雄）who is so unlucky, weak and lazy that his descendants had to send the family robot back in time to help him out. That cat-based robot is DORAEMON, and his four-dimensional pocket produces any number of futuristic gadgets and devices meant to help Nobita become something other than a complete failure in adulthood.

A typical DORAEMON story starts with Nobita suffering from the abuses of class bully nicknamed Gian（技安）, or doing badly in school, coming home crying, and being comforted by a tried but true Doraemon. Doraemon patiently (or resignedly) digs into his four-dimensional pocket and produces a new gadget that (it seems) might offer the perfect cure for any problem, for example, the Wherever Door, which allows one to go anywhere, until Nobita or his friends get too greedy.

DORAEMON acts as the childhood friend or older sibling we all wish we could've had: caring, smarter than us, with a sense of justice, imperfect and fallible enough to not be irritating. Whenever I met with some difficulties in life, I would always wish that I could have my own DORAEMON to give me guidance and help me out.

That is the story I would like to share with you.

★ **Cue card 2 审题训练**

Describe a success you have achieved.

You should say:

What it is.

When it happened.

How you achieved it.

What you can learn from it.

And explain how you felt about it.

✓Joedy 提醒：

如之前说的，成长过程中人们总会遇到成功与失败，考官非常喜欢与考生分享所有快乐的，有趣的以及难忘的经历，所以一般会要求考生讲述"成功"比较多。An experience of success能转到很多不同的变种卡，例如：a piece of good news（成功了，收到好消息）；a happy event（成功了，当然是很快乐了）；an important change / stage in life（也许这次成功就是人生的里程碑呢）；a piece of good advice（成功也许就是因为收到了一条很好的建议啊）。看，很有用的一张卡片，想想吧。写下key words。

★ Cue card 2真题点评与参考答案

I would like to tell you one important success I achieved last semester.

At the end of last semester, I was informed that I got the school scholarship. The moment I got the news, I felt excited although it is not much money. That was recognition of my diligence.

To be honest, I didn't study hard in my academic knowledge in the first two years of my college. At that time, I felt excited because everything for me in the college was fresh and new. I joined some school associations such as students union and took part in all kinds of activities. Besides, I spent a lot of time with my friends and had fun most of the time. I paid more attentions to enriching my life experiences and enjoying my life rather than studying academic knowledge. Finally, it's no doubt that I got an awful score in my final exam.

I was sad and disappointed, even felt shamed for myself. I really wanted to change this awful situation and I couldn't give up myself. So I changed my life style and I began to study hard and put more time and energy on my major courses. Hard work helps me get the scholarship finally.

This process has rebuilt my self-confidence. I believe that nothing is difficult for the man who will try. If I try my best and work hard, I surely could achieve my target. Besides, I also learn that I must believe in myself. If I don't believe in myself, it is hard for others to believe in me.

I will always remember this and this is a milestone in my university life.

Lesson 4 Part 3 听题训练

✓**Joedy** 提醒：

Media and modern technology这个话题几乎贯穿了整个Part 3，毕竟人们现在生活的所有方面都离不开媒体。Part 3把所有的媒体都问过了，包括传统的媒体newspaper, magazine, books, radio；也有现代媒体mobile phones, TV, the Internet等。问题涉及的面非常广，所以大家听题目的时候要注意。好好开声读以下的题目啊。

<table>
<tr><td>

Media

- How beneficial is it to watch TV?

- Is it beneficial for the aged to spend a long time on watching TV?

- Can students attend classes through TV?

- What is the influence of TV on culture?

- What is the difference between the Internet and TV?

- Do you think people will watch more or less TV in the future?

- Which do people prefer, the Internet or the newspapers?

- How do people get news now?

- Can TV programs be educational?

- What are the advantages and disadvantages of sending e-mails?

- Do people in the modern world like using mobile phones or sending e-mails?

- Will letters disappear one day?

- Which is better, handset or mobile phone?

- Which do you like better, sending messages or e-mails?

</td></tr>
</table>

Success

- How do you define success?

- Why do people want to become successful?

- What should people do to achieve success?

- Is the process or the result more important for success?

- What impact does success have on young people?

- What might lead to a person's failure at work?

- Do you think all your efforts should be paid off?

- What is the best reward for a success?

- Is money an important reward?

Lesson 5 Part 3 真题讲解与参考答案

Media

● How beneficial is it to watch TV?

There are lots of benefits of watching TV. The most significant one is that it can relax my body and ease my tension. I especially like watching comedies on TV, which can make me laugh and help me to forget about all the pressure form study or relationship. Listening to some light music from TV can also calm me down from daily life. Besides, watching TV is also a good way to expand my scope of knowledge and widen my vision. I can learn some different interesting things from TV. I always like watching the Discovery Channel. I can learn a lot and it's fun.

✓Joedy 点评：

Watching TV这个话题已经很老土了吧？我们简单总结一下就OK了！

The Good Things About Television

Television is an inescapable part of modern culture that has been brought into the limelight and under heated discussion. Although no absolute agreement has been reached on the topic of TV, we do have to admit the fact that we depend on TV for entertainment, news, education, culture, weather and sports, and television offers lots of benefits to kids, including:

1. Because of its ability to create powerful touchstones, TV enables young people to share cultural experiences with others.

2. Watching TV has become a good occasion for family members to spend some quality time together.

3. When being used skillfully, TV can be a catalyst to get kids reading—following up on TV programs by getting books on the same subjects or reading authors whose works was adapted for the programs. The Harry Porter series can be a perfect example in point.

4. Under parents' guidance, children can develop important values and get life lessons via TV programs.

5. Those controversial or sensitive issues explored in TV programs often make it so much easier for parents and kids to discuss them.

6. Educational programming can develop young children's socialization and learning skills.

7. Factual information like news, current events and historical programming helps to broaden young people's horizon by encouraging them to be more aware of other cultures and people.

8. Documentaries can help develop critical thinking about society and the world.

9. Cultural programming provides young people with easy access to the world of music and art.

✓Joedy 点评：

以上列出的九个电视带来的好处都可以作为考生应试的观点。大家只需要选出比较容易论证的几点，然后加以思考就可以了。注意，并不是说需要面面俱到。相反，抓住一点加以深入论证往往比罗列多个观点要好。

● **Is it beneficial for the aged to spend a long time on watching TV?**

To be honest, I don't think that spending a long time on watching TV is beneficial for the old people. Spending a long time in front of TV may make their life boring and dull. Like my grandparents, they don't like spending too much time on watching TV. They say that sitting on the chair and watching TV too long make their body become stiff and unhealthy. They would like to do some gentle sports such as walking, rather than watching TV for a long time. So I don't think staying in front of TV, watching it all day is good for the aged.

● Can students attend classes through TV?

Definitely, the students can attend classes through TV and I think this is very convenient and efficient for the students to study. I remember in my high school, the teachers always asked us to attend classes through TV at home. We had a flexible schedule at home and felt free. So I think this is also a good way for students to study.

● What is the influence of TV on culture?

Actually, I've never thought about this. Let me see. I think the TV influences the culture in some profound ways. Most of TV programs we are watching now reflect our culture and represent the social value. In return, TV affects our culture too. I remember four years ago, a TV series called Dachangjin from Korea were shown in China. Many Chinese people liked it so much that they followed the ways of cooking and dressing shown in that series. TV helped to bring Korean culture closer to us. So I think TV has great influence on our culture.

● What is the difference between the Internet and TV?

Well, there are many differences between the Internet and TV. The most different thing is that on the Internet we can choose from different information we want. It's very convenient and efficient. However, watching TV is less flexible than surfing on the Internet. All of the programs are stable. We could not change the contents of the programs; we just could change the different channels which we prefer.

● Do you think people will watch more or less TV in the future?

Actually, it's hard to predict that. Let me see. I guess in the future people will be watching TV just as much as now. I don't think that it will change too much in the future. TV is one of the important things in human's life and it is a good way for us to relax and kill time. So I think the time of people spending on TV in the future is just like now. It will not change too much.

● Which do people prefer, the Internet or the newspapers?

In my opinion, it depends. The younger generation, like me, definitely prefers to surf on the Internet, which is easy to access in present day. And almost every young people have their own computer. All of my friends have their own computers. We can find different information which we want on the Internet. It is very convenient and efficient. However, I think the aged prefer newspapers. The main reason is that most of them don't know how to operate the computer, and they find the newspapers easier to access and more flexible, they can read the newspapers on the bus or at home. So I think different people may have different preferences.

● How do people get news now?

There're many methods people can get the news in present day. People can watch TV or read the newspapers and magazines, it's an efficient way to acquire the news especially for most old people. They prefer to use these ways to keep up with the latest development of the society, like my parents. However, the younger generation likes surfing on the Internet. We can find all kinds of information and news from the Internet. I think people would choose to get information from different medias.

● Can TV programs be educational?

Definitely, I think the TV programs can be educational for all people and the TV programs also have responsibility to educate people. Most of young people like me prefer to watch the programs called Discovery. This TV program can introduce to us some interesting things in the world such as some beautiful and interesting animals, just like an encyclopedia. This kind of program can widen our vision and expand our scope of knowledge, making us know the world better and teaching us how to protect the animals. So I think TV programs can be educational.

● What are the advantages and disadvantages of sending e-mails?

Well, let me see. I think the biggest advantage of sending e-mails is that it is more efficient than writing letters. In just 3 to 5 seconds, the person in the other side can receive our information quickly. Beside, I think sending e-mails is quiet environmentally friendly, we don't have to use any paper to write it. It is a good way to preserve the natural resources. However, to some extent, there is an important restriction of sending e-mails. We must not make any mistakes in the e-mail address. If we enter an e-mail address with a wrong letter carelessly, people in the other side could not receive the information forever. This may cause unnecessary losses. So sending e-mails has its advantages and disadvantages.

✓Joedy 点评:

E-mails and letters这个话题今年非常热门，来看看http://wiki.answers.com怎么回答这个

问题的。

What Are Advantages and Disadvantages of E-mail?

In the ten years or so I have been on the Internet I've never seen a disadvantage of using e-mails. They are lightening fast. They won't get lost by the postal services and the person you are sending an e-mail to probably will be thankful that you took the time to send them something through an e-mail such as flowers, a birthday poem rather than sending it through the mail and it reaches who you sent it to on time.

With today's computers and the methods of burning just about anything, you can copy and paste your contact list to Word, print it out, or burn it to a disk where it will be safe.

The advantages of e-mail are:

1. It's fast — Messages can be sent anywhere around the world in an instant.

2. It's cheap — Transmission usually costs nothing, or at the most, very little.

3. It's simple — Easy to use, after initial set-up.

4. It's efficient — Sending to a group can be done in one step.

5. It's versatile — Pictures, power points or other files can be sent too.

The disadvantages are:

1. E-mail can become time-consuming for answering complicated questions and misunderstandings can rise because cultural differences in the interpretation of certain words. The telephone is much better for providing detailed answers or if you feel that the question is not absolutely clear.

2. E-mail can compromise the security of an organization because sensitive information can be easily distributed accidentally or deliberately. E-mail should be entrusted to well-trained and trusted staff members.

3. E-mail can become impersonal or misunderstood.

● Do people in the modern world like using mobile phones or sending e-mails?

Absolutely, most people believe that using mobile phones or sending e-mails is a symbol of keeping up with the modern world. In present days, almost every person has a mobile phone and computer. Both of these two things have become an important part in lives, which could help them to keep closely in touch with their family and friends. Most of my friends told me that their life could not be without mobile phones and e-mails. If they lose their phones, it means they will lose contact with their friends and family. They will lose the sense of safety. So I think both of these two things are very important to the people in modern life and they like to use them.

- Will letters disappear one day?

Actually, it is hard to say! Let me see. I guess letters may not disappear in the future. Although most people prefer to send e-mails, a letter has its own attraction. Let me give you an example, if a boy loves a girl and he wants to tell her, but he is too shy to tell her face to face, I think a handwritten letter is a better option to tell the girl than sending an e-mail. Because most people believe that handwritten letters seem more sincere and persuasive than sending e-mail. So I don't think letters will disappear one day.

✓Joedy 点评：

将来有一天handwritten letters真的会消失吗？看看大家怎么说。

Will Handwritten Letters Disappear Completely?

Handwritten letters have a sense of personal touch, which is much less apparent in cell phone and computer communication. The reason is very simple. Letter writing takes considerably longer time than sending an e-mail on a computer. After finishing a letter, people need to drop it in a mailbox or go to a post office to mail it. In modern time, the idea of spending more time on something indicates the importance attached to it. The recipient of a letter, therefore, appreciates it more than answering a call or getting an e-mail from a friend.

If a guy writes me letters by hand while he is away, and sends them to me, it touches my heart in a way that e-mails do not. There is something about holding a paper in your hand that has traveled from a loved one to you, because their fingers have touched it, and now it's in your hands. Some of what I consider the most romantic couples spent a long time writing each other letters before they could be together. If a guy wrote me a letter every day, I would know he really loves me. I really love to write letters because when I hold a pen in hand, the words that come out are more thoughtful than those I write on a laptop. It has something to do with what Marshall McLuhan said: "The medium is the message."

✓Joedy 点评：

以上这两个参考答案应该是很多中国的考生在第一次听到这个题目时脑海里面想到的观点吧，但是却很少有人能够像答案那样把关于写信最感性的部分描述得如此到位。划线部分的表达都很值得大家参考。

For sure. As time goes by, new generations of children perhaps won't even learn how to format a written letter. The big disadvantage of them is that it is slower than e-mails.

I don't really think there is a way of stopping this. Science can't be stopped. If we simply accept that technology is a way of making our lives easier, eventually, things as letters will disappear. What could be done is to educate people about how an e-mail could be. What I mean is to make an e-mail similar and formatted the same way as a letter should be. only in this way, can we have the formality and the importance of letters together with the speed of an e-mail.

✓Joedy 点评：

这是一个很精彩的答案。在观点方面，该考生能够打破常规，不去论证某一方的好处或者坏处，而是建议把e-mail和letter的好处融合在一起，答案显得滴水不漏；在语言方面，能够自如地运用包括条件状语从句（第二段第二句），主语从句（第二段第三、四句）以及倒装句（第二段最后一句）等精彩句型。

● **Which is better, handset or mobile phone?**

In my opinion, both handset and mobile phone have their advantages and disadvantages. But for me, I prefer mobile phones because a mobile phone is more convenient and flexible than a handset. I can answer the mobile phone everywhere I want, including outside and at home. Whereas the handset can just be used at home or in the office, it's very restricted by the distance. So I think the mobile phone is better than the handset.

● **Which do you like better, sending messages or e-mails?**

Well, in my mind, I prefer sending messages than an e-mails. Because, to some extent, I think sending messages is easier and more convenient than e-mails. All of my friends have mobile phones in present day, all of them can receive my messages quickly. However, it does not mean that all of them possess computers, you know, a computer is more expensive than a mobile phone and some of them could not afford it. So they could not receive my e-mails. Because of this, I like sending messages better.

Success

● **How do you define success?**

In my opinion, success means that achieving my target as well as my parents and friends have recognized my achievement. This can make me feel happy and satisfactory. To be brief, when I feel happy, I think I succeed. Actually, success is quite simple for me and I'm easy to be satisfied.

✓Joedy 点评：

成功是个很抽象的概念，看看一些成功的人是如何定义成功的。

What Is Success and How Do We Achieve It?

To be clear about what success is must be the first step to achieve success.

So far, the best definition I have come across is: "Success is the completion of anything intended." In other words success is finishing what you planned to do.

Even robbing a bank is a kind of success if that is what you wished to do. However, you probably did not intend to end up in prison!

The above definition of success shines a light on failure and success. Make a plan and follow it and you will have succeeded. Make a plan and do not follow it and you will have failed.

This gives a yard stick for judging every day of our lives. We can say at the end of the day "I have failed" or "I have succeeded."

This may seem very obvious but it is amazing that only about 85% of the human race end up doing what they intended to.

I asked several people what they thought success was. One person said that "Success is making loads of money." Another said that success is "Achieving your goals". Someone else said that success is "Fulfilling your potential". An interesting answer was that success is "Making others jealous".

Brian Tracy agrees with the connection between success and goals. He has said "Success is goals, and all else is commentary." Tracy believes that people with clear, written goals, accomplish far more in a shorter period of time than people without them.

A great quote by Jim Ryun, the American Athlete, is as follows.

"Motivation is what gets you started. Habit is what keeps you going".

Another brilliant quote is:

"Try not to become a man of success but rather try to become a man of value.", by Albert Einstein.

The next quote says more or less the same thing:

"Success usually comes to those who are too busy to be looking for it.", by Henry David Thoreau.

Success then is putting in 100% effort whatever the results are. More often than not, however, the results will be excellent.

Michael Angier has a great definition of success.

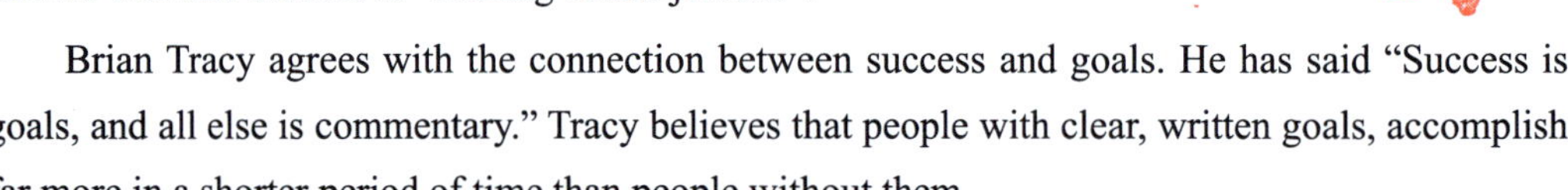

"Success is the result of steadily taking action on our most important goals. When we consistently focus our energies and our efforts upon what matters most, we can't help but be successful."

● **Why do people want to become successful?**

Well, let me see. Actually, it's hard to say. But I firmly believe that every person wants to be successful in their life. I think when one becomes successful, he or she can easily get more wealth and more satisfaction of life. They can gain recognition from their peers and family. Like my uncle, he is a successful individual in the business and he is very wealthy. My whole family appreciates him very much and recognizes his achievement totally. He has a great life. So I think both wealth and recognition are the most principal reasons people want to become successful.

● **What should people do to achieve success?**

In my opinion, if someone wants to be successful, he or she should make lots of efforts in life. First of all, they should be diligent and study hard in their business. If they are lazy as well as unmotivated, they are hardly likely to achieve their target. And I firmly believe that nothing is difficult for the man who will try. Besides, persistence is another important factor for success. My mother always says to me, if you give up in the half way, you will never gain success. So in my mind, if people want to achieve success, they should be diligent and persistent.

✓Joedy 点评：

要怎么做才能成功呢？看看wikiHow: http://wikihow.com如何教大家。

How to Become a Success

There may not be one secret to success, but there are certain things most successful people do. Follow this process and you will have all the success you desire.

1. Get into a positive mindset. Spend time each day to appreciate all the things you have. When you wake up, feel grateful that you have been given another day. When you're driving to work, be grateful for the roads and the car that gets you there. When you arrive at work, be grateful for your co-workers who enlighten your day and make your job easier. When you have your lunch, be grateful for the food you have been given. Soon, these feelings of gratitude will become a part of you and your path to success will be a bright one. Many people tend to focus on the negative things in their life and thus they are given more negative things. When you fill yourself with positive feelings, more positive things are attracted to you.

2. Visualize the things you want. Close your eyes and visualize you already having it. Feel the feelings of already having it. The law of attraction will begin the creative process of forming that thought into a thing, a reality. Your subconscious will become more aware of opportunities that will bring you the things you think about.

3. Have faith in what you can do. Martin Luther King Jr. said it best: "Take the first step of faith, you don't have to see it, you just have to take it." Recognize doubt and reverse it with faith.

4. Take action. Do all that can be done everyday. That said, know when you're trying to do too much, you want to be efficient, not stressed all the time. You can not act in the past or future so focus your actions in your present space.

5. Learn from your past experience, and try not to repeat your mistakes. If you were not successful in achieving something earlier then, analyze the reasons for your failure, please don't cry over a spilled milk, it's already on the floor, go and get some new milk.

再来看看另外一个版本的说法。

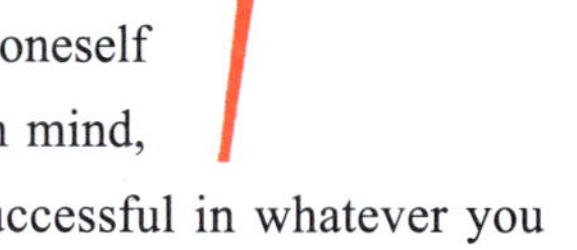

How to Be Successful

Many people want to achieve success in life, but it's easier said than done. There are so many distractions that it can be challenging to discipline oneself to accomplish a monumental goal. By keeping the following advice in mind, however, you can dramatically increase your chances of becoming successful in whatever you choose to pursue.

1. Define the meaning of success as you see it. You cannot have success if you do not know what it means for you. Everyone views success differently. Set clear goals and be realistic. How will you know when you've achieved your goals? Your standards should be quantifiable, or else you could spend your entire life chasing after a vague goal. For example, let's say you want to be good at your job. You get a promotion, you get a raise, but you still haven't reached your goal because you could always do better, right? You could always get promoted even further, or make even more money. Whatever you have will never be enough. Instead, create benchmarks: "My goal is to increase my productivity by 30% and only be late for work five times per year, at the most." These are quantifiable goals that when achieved, give you a sense of satisfaction and completion, making you feel successful and confident.

2. Study successful people. Look around — who has the success that you envision for yourself? What are they doing? How do they approach life? Become their apprentice. Ask them for advice. Spend time around them, if you can, learn from them.

3. Take risks. Step out of your comfort zone. Successful people think big and act big. It can be a scary thing to do, but if you don't, then will you ever be successful? Don't wait for opportunities to fall in your lap. Sniff them out. Successful people make big investments (in their careers, in their businesses, in their education) and all investments involve risk. But don't be reckless. Study your risks, make sure the odds are in your favor, then take a leap. Be bold.

4. Solve problems. People who are successful encourage progress by solving problems and answering questions. No matter where you are or what you're doing, look around and try and think of ways you can contribute. What are people struggling with or complaining about? How can you make life easier for them in an effective way? Can you re-design or re-organize some aspect of the situation so that things run more smoothly? Can you create a product or provide a service that fills a critical gap? Be proactive and resourceful.

5. Be persistent. Don't give up. If your first attempt didn't work, don't quit. When asked about his 10,000 failed attempts to develop a storage battery, the prolific American inventor Thomas Edison responded: "I have not failed, I've just found 10,000 ways that won't work."

6. Remember that success does not guarantee happiness. Success is equated with the achievement of a goal, but don't assume it will always bring happiness. Many people make the mistake that if they accomplish this or that, they'll be happier, but fulfillment and satisfaction have a lot more to do with how you approach life than with what you do in life. Keep that in perspective.

✓Joedy 提醒：

看完了这么多成功的tips，大家是否有了自己明确的选择呢？我在这里提供给大家的是一些参考的方案，具体如何选择还是看大家个人。当然，大家也可以综合以上我们的意见，这就是给大家提供这么多背景参考资料的初衷了。

● Is the process or the result more important for success?

Well, I think the process is absolutely more important than the result for success. Unfortunately, most people focus on the result, like my parents. I am studying hard to achieve my target, which is also my parents' expectation. However, sometimes, the result was not as how they expected. They felt unhappy and disappointed. It also makes me full of pressure and I become unmotivated as well as nervous. I really hope that they can pay more attention to the process rather than the result.

● What impact does success have on young people?

Actually, I've never thought about this. Let me see. Well, in my mind, I think the best influence of success on young people is to stimulate them to get further study and work hard in their industry. They will try their best to achieve the next success. As a matter of fact, success is kind of social recognition for young people. If they achieve success in their field, to some extent, they will be happy and full of energy and passion in their research.

● What might lead to a person's failure at work?

In my opinion, not enough perseverance is the most principal reason that leads to failure. My mother always says to me, if you give up in the half way, you will never be successful. And I firmly believe that if we insist our ideal and work hard for it, we will be successful one day, although I feel tired in the half way sometimes. By contract, my cousin, he learned how to play the piano in his childhood, but he gave up in his half way because he had no persistence. Finally, he gave it up and failed in this field. So I think not enough perseverance is the most principal reason that leads to failure.

● Do you think all your efforts should be paid off?

Actually, it's hard to say. Different people may have different answers to this question. But for me, I don't think all the efforts should be paid off. If I always want to be paid off in my every effort, I will not be happy and feel disappointed because most of time my efforts are not paid off. Of course, if my efforts have been paid off, I will surely feel happy and pleased, but if no, I may not feel disappointed. Actually, it's very hard to define that.

● What is the best reward for a success?

Well, it's hard to say because different people have different answer to this question. Some people think that money is the best reward for a success while others deem that a sense of achievement and recognition is more important than the money for a success. But for me, I think both money and reputation are an equally significant reward for a success. Money can sustain their life as well as inspiring them to get further research, whereas great reputation can offer them a sense of satisfaction and achievement. So I think both of money and reputation are the best reward for a success.

● Is money an important reward?

Yes, I think money is one of the important rewards for many people. Undoubtedly, they also can gain a sense of achievement in the reward. In fact, many people try their best to achieve the reward just for the money. Because enough money could help them to sustain the life and make further research in their business. Besides, money as reward is also a kind of inspiration. It can encourage people to work hard and make more contributions to the society. So I think money is an important reward.

致"烤鸭"后语

亲爱的"烤鸭"们：

经过近一年的编写，我的《轻松备战雅思口语》终于定稿了。

感激这一年，让我能在忙碌的上课间隙寻找到安静思考的空间；感激这一年，让混乱已久的头绪慢慢地沉淀下来；感激这一年，给予我在未来的无数年努力向前的勇气！

不得不承认，编写的过程是痛苦的，经过不断的思考、不断的自我否定以及不断的修改，我总想让这本书变得更好一点更能帮助"烤鸭"们多一点。编写的过程也是快乐的，当一个新idea涌进脑海，当发掘到一些对"烤鸭"们有用的材料时，我又会感到无限的狂喜……

希望各位"烤鸭"能充分利用我在本书里提供的所有有用的素材，做好充分的准备以迎战雅思；希望大家的备考过程是快乐的，有收获的；希望大家所有的努力都能有所回报！

最后，送大家一段我很喜欢的话，加油咯！

Believe while others are doubting.

Plan while others are playing.

Study while others are sleeping.

Decide while others are delaying.

Prepare while others are daydreaming.

Work while others are wishing.

Save while others are wasting.

Listen while others are talking.

Smile while others are pouting.

Commend while others are criticizing.

Persist while others are quitting.

Joedy

2010年6月